PRESENTING THE PAST

ARCHAEOLOGIST'S TOOLKIT

SERIES EDITORS: LARRY J. ZIMMERMAN AND WILLIAM GREEN

The Archaeologist's Toolkit is an integrated set of seven volumes designed to teach novice archaeologists and students the basics of doing archaeological fieldwork, analysis, and presentation. Students are led through the process of designing a study, doing survey work, excavating, properly working with artifacts and biological remains, curating their materials, and presenting findings to various audiences. The volumes—written by experienced field archaeologists— are full of practical advice, tips, case studies, and illustrations to help the reader. All of this is done with careful attention to promoting a conservation ethic and an understanding of the legal and practical environment of contemporary American cultural resource laws and regulations. The Toolkit is an essential resource for anyone working in the field and ideal for training archaeology students in classrooms and field schools.

Volume 1: *Archaeology by Design*
By Stephen L. Black and Kevin Jolly

Volume 2: *Archaeological Survey*
By James M. Collins and Brian Leigh Molyneaux

Volume 3: *Excavation*
By David L. Carmichael and Robert Lafferty

Volume 4: *Artifacts*
By Charles R. Ewen

Volume 5: *Archaeobiology*
By Kristin D. Sobolik

**Volume 6: *Curating Archaeological Collections:
From the Field to the Repository***
By Lynne P. Sullivan and S. Terry Childs

Volume 7: *Presenting the Past*
By Larry J. Zimmerman

PRESENTING THE PAST

LARRY J. ZIMMERMAN

ARCHAEOLOGIST'S TOOLKIT
VOLUME 7

ALTAMIRA
PRESS

A Division of Rowman & Littlefield Publishers, Inc.
Walnut Creek • Lanham • New York • Oxford

For Karen Zimmerman, who more than
thirty years ago pointed out that archaeology
is mostly science fiction. She was right.

AltaMira Press
A Division of Rowman & Littlefield Publishers, Inc.
1630 North Main Street, #367
Walnut Creek, CA 94596
www.altamirapress.com

Rowman & Littlefield Publishers, Inc.
A Division of Rowman & Littlefield Publishers, Inc.
4501 Forbes Boulevard, Suite 200
Lanham, MD 20706

PO Box 317
Oxford
OX2 9RU, UK

British Library Cataloguing in Publication Information Available

Library of Congress Cataloging-in-Publication Data

Zimmerman, Larry J. 1947–
    Presenting the past / Larry J. Zimmerman
    p. cm.—(The archaeologist's toolkit ; v. 7)
    Includes bibliographical references (p.) and index.
    ISBN 0-7591-0403-4 (cloth : alk. paper) — ISBN 0-7591-0025-X (pbk. : alk.
paper)
    1. Archaeology—Methodology. 2. Archaeology—Public relations. 3. Communication
of technical information—Handbooks, manuals, etc. 4. Communication of technical
information—Audio-visual aids. 5. Public speaking—Handbooks, manuals, etc. 6.
Report writing—Handbooks, manuals, etc. I. Title. II. Series.

    CC75.7 .Z56 2003
    808'.06693—dc21   2002152407

Printed in the United States of America

♾™ The paper used in this publication meets the minimum requirements of American
National Standard for Information Sciences—Permanence of Paper for Printed Library
Materials, ANSI/NISO Z39.48–1992.

 CONTENTS

CDs/DVDs • Interactivity: Bringing the Past to Life •
Conclusion

SERIES EDITORS' FOREWORD

The Archaeologist's Toolkit is a series of books on how to plan, design, carry out, and use the results of archaeological research. The series contains seven books written by acknowledged experts in their fields. Each book is a self-contained treatment of an important element of modern archaeology. Therefore, each book can stand alone as a reference work for archaeologists in public agencies, private firms, and museums, as well as a textbook and guidebook for classrooms and field settings. The books function even better as a set, because they are integrated through cross-references and complementary subject matter.

Archaeology is a rapidly growing field, one that is no longer the exclusive province of academia. Today, archaeology is a part of daily life in both the public and private sectors. Thousands of archaeologists apply their knowledge and skills every day to understand the human past. Recent explosive growth in archaeology has heightened the need for clear and succinct guidance on professional practice. Therefore, this series supplies ready reference to the latest information on methods and techniques—the tools of the trade that serve as handy guides for longtime practitioners and essential resources for archaeologists in training.

Archaeologists help solve modern problems: They find, assess, recover, preserve, and interpret the evidence of the human past in light of public interest and in the face of multiple land use and development interests. Most of North American archaeology is devoted to cultural resource management (CRM), so the Archaeologist's Toolkit focuses on practical approaches to solving real problems in CRM and public archaeology. The books contain numerous case studies from all parts of the continent, illustrating the range and diversity of applications. The series emphasizes the importance of such realistic considerations as budgeting, scheduling, and team coordination. In addition, accountability to the public as well as to the profession is a common theme throughout the series.

Volume 1, *Archaeology by Design*, stresses the importance of research design in all phases and at all scales of archaeology. It shows how and why you should develop, apply, and refine research designs. Whether you are surveying quarter-acre cell tower sites or excavating stratified villages with millions of artifacts, your work will be more productive, efficient, and useful if you pay close and continuous attention to your research design.

Volume 2, *Archaeological Survey*, recognizes that most fieldwork in North America is devoted to survey: finding and evaluating archaeological resources. It covers prefield and field strategies to help you maximize the effectiveness and efficiency of archaeological survey. It shows how to choose appropriate strategies and methods ranging from landowner negotiations, surface reconnaissance, and shovel testing to geophysical survey, aerial photography, and report writing.

Volume 3, *Excavation*, covers the fundamentals of dirt archaeology in diverse settings, while emphasizing the importance of ethics during the controlled recovery—and destruction—of the archaeological record. This book shows how to select and apply excavation methods appropriate to specific needs and circumstances and how to maximize useful results while minimizing loss of data.

Volume 4, *Artifacts*, provides students as well as experienced archaeologists with useful guidance on preparing and analyzing artifacts. Both prehistoric and historic-era artifacts are covered in detail. The discussion and case studies range from processing and cataloging through classification, data manipulation, and specialized analyses of a wide range of artifact forms.

Volume 5, *Archaeobiology*, covers the analysis and interpretation of biological remains from archaeological sites. The book shows how to recover, sample, analyze, and interpret the plant and animal remains most frequently excavated from archaeological sites in North America. Case studies from CRM and other archaeological research illustrate strategies for effective and meaningful use of biological data.

Volume 6, *Curating Archaeological Collections*, addresses a crucial but often ignored aspect of archaeology: proper care of the specimens and records generated in the field and the lab. This book covers strategies for effective short- and long-term collections management. Case studies illustrate the do's and don'ts that you need to know in order to make the best use of existing collections and to make your own work useful for others.

Volume 7, *Presenting the Past*, covers another area that has not received sufficient attention: communication of archaeology to a variety of audiences. Different tools are needed to present archaeology to other archaeologists, to sponsoring agencies, and to the interested public. This book shows how to choose the approaches and methods to take when presenting technical and nontechnical information through various means to various audiences.

Each of these books and the series as a whole are designed to be equally useful to practicing archaeologists and to archaeology students. Practicing archaeologists in CRM firms, agencies, academia, and museums will find the books useful as reference tools and as brush-up guides on current concerns and approaches. Instructors and students in field schools, lab classes, and short courses of various types will find the series valuable because of each book's practical orientation to problem solving.

As the series editors, we have enjoyed bringing these books together and working with the authors. We thank all of the authors—Steve Black, Dave Carmichael, Terry Childs, Jim Collins, Charlie Ewen, Kevin Jolly, Robert Lafferty, Brian Molyneaux, Kris Sobolik, and Lynne Sullivan—for their hard work and patience. We also offer sincere thanks to Mitch Allen of AltaMira Press and a special acknowledgment to Brian Fagan.

LARRY J. ZIMMERMAN
WILLIAM GREEN

ACKNOWLEDGMENTS

This book derives from many discussions and arguments with colleagues about how best to tell people what we find and do. Larry Bradley, Rich Fox, Brian Molyneaux, and other staff members of the University of South Dakota Archaeology Laboratory have always been good sounding boards and full of good ideas, and always willing to tell each other in good-natured ways that we were "full of it." Colleagues on the SAA Committee on Ethics provided a wide range of ideas, and the insights gained from the committee's 2000 and 2001 sessions on the media were especially useful. John Doershuk, Claire Smith, Tristine Smart, Joe Watkins, Alison Wylie, Randy McGuire, Kris Hirst, Shirley Schermer, Lynn Alex, and many others shared lots of insight and experiences to help form many of my ideas. My coeditor for the Archaeologist's Toolkit series, Bill Green, has been an extraordinary colleague and friend. Mitch Allen is a profoundly patient man who exemplifies what a good editor should be. Because this book is partly about publishing, his insights proved to be extremely valuable. Thanks to you all.

Finally, I'd like to thank Karen Zimmerman, who has put up with my whining for years.

1

OUT OF SITE, OUT OF MIND?

Once upon a time in archaeology, grizzled, field-hardened professors told their students that "you aren't a real archaeologist unless you die with at least one unfinished site report." The press of salvage archaeology and the heady, money-dripping days of early CRM projects hardly left time to do more than get artifacts out of the ground and dash on to survey the next sewage lagoon or bridge replacement. An awful truth exacerbated these time pressures: Many of us who got into archaeology did so because it was the fieldwork and its discoveries that excited us more than anything else. The lab was always a distant second choice for us and mostly boring. The rare exception came when some new technology became available to allow us bit of analytical or interpretive wizardry.

When it came to actually writing up the project, the pain really started. Writing was a cold bucket of water dousing the flames of passion for the field. To be sure, some proved bold and daring enough to throw together a conference paper, usually outlined on the plane on the way to the conference or in the hotel room the night before a "yawner" of an 8 A.M. session. A few brazenly went so far as to turn their work into a monograph read by a few dozen colleagues or a journal article skimmed by a few hundred, provoking envy from many and establishing celebrity for some.

Accountability to a range of publics changed all that. Pesky contract managers who paid the bills for some federal or state agency started to hound us for reports so that they could jump through legislative and regulatory hoops. Deep down, we knew that the reports just lined a bookshelf or engorged a file drawer in some minion's office. Were the deadlines really all that important? To make matters worse, somebody came up with the bright idea that the folks who really paid the bills— taxpayers or shareholders—might actually be interested in what we were finding with the contract dollars their congressional delegates or CEOs always seemed so hesitant to spend. They wanted us to write public reports and articles for popular magazines, set up traveling exhibits, and present agency-sponsored projects in a way the public could understand.

To top it all off, modern archaeology, with its emphasis on multidisciplinary approaches, brought with it the complexities of collaborative projects. Single-authored, jargon-laden, mostly descriptive reports were no longer acceptable even to colleagues, let alone CRM bureaucrats. Our professional organizations went so far as to codify the idea that we ought to write up our fieldwork.

Unfortunately, the truth of the matter is that many archaeological projects do go unreported, for a variety of reasons, including a lack of time and funding, difficulties interpreting complex cultural remains, and fear of professional criticism. British archaeologist Peter Addyman claims that up to 60 percent of modern excavations go unpublished after ten years, and only 10 percent of excavations funded by the National Science Foundation since 1950 ever reached print. In Israel the problems are worse, with about 39 percent of the excavations from the 1960s, 75 percent in the 1970s, and 87 percent in the 1980s going unreported (Renfrew and Bahn 1996:535–36).

Most of us also learned along the way that archaeology is a destructive process. Our excavations can wreck a site as completely as a bulldozer or a chisel plow. That's why most of us fully realize the need to report our excavations. If we don't, and the artifacts just sit on a shelf in our labs, we've just contributed to site destruction. If we think carefully about it, we should fully understand the problem and have a profoundly guilty conscience about any sites we've dug that we haven't reported.

If the past is a public heritage, as many archaeologists consider it to be, when we don't report a site we've dug, we commit a double theft. We've first stolen from the people paying the bills and then from the public of whose heritage we say we are the stewards. We become little different from the looters we condemn who dig up artifacts to sell for profit in the lucrative antiquities market.

MAKING EXCUSES

The reasons we don't get the work written up can be many, starting with our own attitudes toward writing, but often, we just don't allow ourselves time or budget to get the job done. We can make excuses about how tough it is to convince a contract manager whose eye is always on the bottom line that it really does take about triple or greater the amount of time in the lab as it does in the field to get analysis, interpretation, and write-up done. We constantly tell our students this in textbooks and lectures, but why don't we make the same effort to educate the bean counters?

We also make excuses about how our labs don't have the best equipment or the latest version of our favorite word-processing software, but we ought to be ashamed of ourselves. Ludmila Koryakova of the Laboratory of Archaeological Researches at Ural State University told me of how Russian archaeologists often struggle to stay ahead of rampant site destruction, with relatively few resources at their disposal. Site reports often get handwritten in pencil, with only one copy of the report in existence because they don't have copiers! She lives in fear that the single copies will somehow be lost and all records of important sites destroyed forever. When I gave her an old laptop computer, she was ecstatic!

If we put aside our own lethargy and excuse making, we may notice something we might truly lack, and that is adequate training to prepare our reports. Although many archaeology texts describe the need to report our work, they rarely give any clue as to how difficult this task is or to the tools or strategies for actually doing it. Few of us can recall any courses specifically geared to writing our reports or presenting our materials. Although we probably took part in field and lab methods classes, studied topical issues or culture areas, and lived and slept theory, almost no one was taught anything about presenting the past. We were somehow to learn this by reading other reports, or by listening to colleagues give conference papers, or by figuring it all out by osmosis. This may be a major failing of our educational system in archaeology.

Another problem for us is that at least since the 1950s, archaeology very much has been a multidisciplinary team effort. For our excavations and analyses, we require many specialists, as noted in the other books in this series. We need our geomorphologists and archaeobiologists in the field with us. We need them in the lab, too, where they might handle analysis on everything from sediment particle size to gas chromatography on charred residue in pottery. Although we know full well that the days of a professor, three graduate students, and a cloud of dust are over, many of us still see what we do as a more or less solitary venture. Some of us work in very small CRM firms, and we rely on contracting out much of our specialty labor. We might get a report from our consultant, but it's up to us to massage it into our final reports. Others of us work in a university system where joint publications are unfortunately not given the same weight toward tenure and promotion that single-authored books, monographs, and papers might be. The result is that we tend to see production of our reports as a mostly solitary chore when it should often be a team production.

Finally, and paradoxically, archaeologists are prodigious borrowers. We can bend almost any theoretical approach to our wishes, and we easily latch onto new technologies for field and laboratory work. However, when it comes to preparing and presenting our reports, we have been slow to adjust to new media. Many of us are still firmly hooked on hard copy when more appropriate media are readily available for everything from site reports to books like this one!

PLAN OF THE BOOK

The intent of this book is to provide you with basic tools you'll need to present the past. Topics will be wide-ranging, sometimes reading like a primer but also providing resources if you have already mastered the basics. Chapter 2 considers archaeology's audiences and how to recognize them. Chapter 3 is geared toward helping you decide on the media you'll use to meet audience, personal, and budgetary needs for your presentation. Chapter 4 looks at basic writing skills and how to develop them, and it also considers some of the complexities of writing such as style, jargon, and dealing with references. Chapter 5 takes a brief look at computers and software, more about their use than the specifics of hardware and software. Chapter 6 considers visual archaeology, the creation and use of images in our presentations, from drawings to video. Chapter 7 examines team approaches to presenting the past. Chapters 8 and 9 essentially start with presentations of various kinds, from conference papers and luncheon talks, and move to the world of publishing, from peer review to working with editors. Chapter 10 looks at alternative ways to bring the past to life, from exhibits and events to cartoons and movies. Chapter 11 shows how you can work with the media to publicize the past. Chapter 12 deals with new technologies and how we will present the past in the future.

There is structure to this. In one sense, the book follows what might be considered the processes of presenting the past; that is, the text moves from looking at audiences to selecting materials for them, to preparing and delivering the materials. Another thread linking chapters is the kinds of presentations or media available to us, from presentations to digital technologies. As complex as this approach might seem, much derives from a few key issues.

The starting point for the rest of this book is a single question: For whom do we do archaeology? However you answer the question, your answer(s) dictate how you present the past. Archaeology has a wide range of constituencies, including both colleagues and the public, so effective presentation of the past needs to begin with the differences in audiences.

RECOGNIZING OUR AUDIENCES

The single greatest problem in presenting the past may be figuring out who our audience is. Many of us never even think about the problem that can be. Professionally we are an odd lot. As archaeologist and essayist Loren Eisley (1971:81) observed in his book *The Night Country*, "A man [sic] who has looked with the archaeological eye will never quite see normally again." To a degree, we pride ourselves in our peculiar viewpoint. Those of us who consider ourselves first to be anthropologists should recognize that anthropologists are often marginal to their own societies. We never really quite fit in. Sociocultural anthropologists, at least according to the popular stereotype, study the Other, that exotic, non-Western member of a small-scale society living in one of the world's remote locales. At least anthropologists study living people, but we archaeologists study cultures long gone, where we don't even have to deal with the living, who just tend to get in the way. To paraphrase L. P. Hartley (1953:xvi) in *The Go Between*, the past becomes our foreign country.

To a degree we revel in our marginality and isolation, and we certainly get along best with our own kind. I don't mean this in a negative or harshly critical way; both actually have their utility for our field- and lab work. Still, these characteristics can get in our way when it comes to communicating what we do. Although our relative isolation as a profession can provide a modicum of comfort, most archaeologists realize that they do not do their work in a vacuum. During the past three decades, with the rise of cultural resources management (CRM) and the advocacy of a wide range of publics for some level of control of what they consider to be their own pasts, archaeologists have come to understand the very public nature of what we do. In recognition, the Society for American Archaeology (SAA) spent several years in the early 1990s developing an ethics code, many segments of which are geared toward communication with colleagues and various publics, as well as how to educate our students to do so.

ETHICS AND ACCOUNTABILITY

During the early 1990s, the SAA began a series of deliberations, small conferences, and open-member comment on how the society might revise its ethics code (see Lynott and Wylie 1995). The Executive Committee of the SAA approved the code in 1996 (see Principles of Archaeological Ethics at www.saa.org/Aboutsaa/Ethics/prethic.html to read the code). The principle of stewardship of the past in both practice and promotion is at the core of the code, and there is some level of recognition of the discipline's publics in virtually every principle. Certainly Principle No. 2, "Accountability," directly recognizes our links to other communities, as does Principle No. 4, "Public Education and Outreach." Principle No. 6, "Public Reporting and Publication," brings it all home in terms of this book. As part of the principle states, "Within a reasonable time, the knowledge archaeologists gain from investigation of the archaeological record must be presented in accessible form (through publication or other means) to as wide a range of interested publics as possible."

EDUCATING OUR STUDENTS

Soon thereafter, the SAA's Education Committee began a lengthy examination of the ways in which archaeologists educate their students, culminating in a substantial report, *Teaching Archaeology in the 21st Century* (Bender and Smith 2000), in which they outlined several "Principles for Curriculum Reform." Presentation of the past is clearly mentioned in two of them, along with possible topics for consideration in student training:

- *"Written and Oral Communication."* Archaeology depends on the understanding and support of the public. For this to occur, archaeologists must communicate their goals, results, and recommendations clearly and effectively. Archaeology training must incorporate training and frequent practice in logical thinking as well as written and oral presentation. Possible topics: Clear writing (implied clear thinking), clear speaking, public speaking, computer literacy.

- *"Basic Archaeological Skills."* Students planning on a career in archaeology must have mastered a set of basic cognitive and methodological skills that enable them to operate effectively in the field and laboratory contexts. These skills must span the range of basic professional responsibility: excavation, analysis, report writing, and long term curation. Possible topics: Observation skills, inferential skills, basic map skills, organizing and assessing data, knowledge of the law, technical writing.

The "Written and Oral Communication" principle is fairly direct about the importance of communicating well to our publics. As important, the principle states that students should be trained in how to do it. The "Basic Archaeological Skills" principle specifically mentions writing for colleagues. Between the SAA Ethics Code and the principles regarding archaeology education, there can be no doubt that communicating the past well and to a range of publics is extremely important.

PUBLIC ACCOUNTABILITY: WHAT DO DIFFERENT AUDIENCES WANT AND NEED?

Few archaeologists would disagree that the past is important and that archaeology can be a powerful tool for understanding it. Most would probably agree that the scientific method behind archaeology is probably the greatest contribution of the Western tradition to world heritage. At the same time, "science is a very human form of knowledge" (Bronowski 1973:374). Scientists want to "proselytize" the public as much as any other belief system does in order to make them think like we do. We archaeologists tend to be offended when others don't think the past is as important as we think it is, when what they do might "destroy" a past we hold so dear. We work hard in our public education programs to show our publics how important it is and why they should support preservation, or at least conservation, of the past. However, do we really know what our publics think?

A coalition of archaeological organizations, including the SAA, the Archaeological Conservancy, the Archaeological Institute of America, the Bureau of Land Management, the Fish and Wildlife Service, the

Forest Service, the National Park Service, and the Society for Historical Archaeology, used a Harris poll to determine how Americans view
archaeology. A random sample of 1,016 adults across the continental
United States answered questions about the public's grasp of, and participation in, archaeology (SAA 2000). The SAA's press release summary of the poll shows that "a majority (60%) of the public believes in
the value to society of archaeological research and education."

The devil is in the details, however. Although nearly everyone felt
there should be laws protecting archaeological resources, when it came
to laws about resources on private land, there was a 16 percent drop,
from 96 percent to 80 percent in support. When it came to removing archaeological objects from a foreign country without permission, 64 percent said this should not happen. There is some confusion about the role
of archaeologists, with a tendency to link archaeology to recent discoveries. When it came to how people learned about archaeology:

> The majority of respondents learned about archaeology through televi-
> sion (56%) and books, encyclopedias, and magazines (33%), followed by
> newspapers (24%). Learning about archaeology in school accounted for
> 23% of respondents at the college level, 20% at the secondary level, and
> 10% at the primary level, although the vast majority (90%) believed that
> students should learn about archaeology as part of the school curricu-
> lum from their earliest years. Most of the public (88%) have visited a
> museum exhibiting archaeological material, while 1 in 3 people (37%)
> have visited an archaeological site. (SAA 2000)

For most of the public, however, the primary use of archaeology is
probably for entertainment. Certainly people think the past is important, until it gets in the way of their ownership, their job, or their pet
project. The fact that the two largest media for learning about it are
television and museum visits should tell us something important: If
we want to get our messages across to the public, we need to find
ways to teach that are entertaining *and* intellectually enlightening. If
you doubt that others feel this way, read Brian Fagan's (2002) diatribe
"I Am So Tired of Jargon and Narrow Teaching . . ." in the *SAA Archaeological Record*.

Think about what got you into archaeology in the first place. More
than likely, you read or saw on television some popularized story
about a discovery. For those from an era when television was limited,
it might have been a book such as C. W. Ceram's *Gods, Graves, and
Scholars;* if you are younger, you might have gotten pulled in by the
Ice Man in the Alps or even a movie like *Raiders of the Lost Ark*.

When you took your first academic classes, you began to understand that learning academic archaeology was work; entertainment was no longer so important. If your first dig was in a hot Iowa cornfield working on a "culture of poverty" lithic scatter, you learned that the romance of archaeology flies very quickly. As you became a professional, something deeper kept you going, perhaps the chance of discovery or some intangible quality of field- and lab work. Fun, yes, but hardly the sort of fun most of the public likes!

On a more serious level, we also need to learn that archaeology can be a very cruel discipline. Like history, archaeology can literally undercut a people's belief system. Little wonder that many tradition-oriented American Indians despise an archaeology that sometimes seeks to debunk their origin stories. The problem, of course, is how to deal with archaeological interpretations about the past and our kind of "truth" versus a concern for people's feelings. That is no small matter!

We shouldn't have to dumb down everything we do so that it "sells" or makes people "feel good" about themselves. Rather, we had better figure out that just doing archaeological reports doesn't cut it if we want our publics to learn about, let alone buy into, our disciplinary views about the past. Worse, it may even alienate them if done without sensitivity to their concerns or needs. Except for all of us liking the exciting elements of discovery—the newest, the oldest, and the greatest—archaeology's is an exceedingly difficult message. By its very nature, archaeology has problems in dealing with the individual in the past (except, of course, in historical archaeology where there may be documentary evidence). We deal with the material results of cultural norms. We are forced to objectify, and that often takes the "humanity" out of our work. With the human side gone, what we write is often boring. Even most archaeologists have a tough time reading the 105th description of a potsherd in a report or looking at the eighth chart of a factor analysis. If we can figure out ways to put people back into our work, we have a better chance of success. There *is* fascinating archaeology out there, and it sells!

As an archaeologist, you need to make sure that you understand this point. Yes, you must write reports for your contracting agency in CRM and for your colleagues. Be aware, however, that if the discipline is truly accountable to the public and ever hopes to accomplish anything remotely related to public education, we must recognize the need for different kinds of presentations of the past. We have to work diligently to find ways of presenting the past that are sensitive to the wants and needs of our publics.

ARCHAEOLOGICAL STYLE AND THE REAL WORLD

To do this sort of presentation of the past, we need to consider our own attitudes. Although the following may seem like "preachy" statements from a bully pulpit, some reflection on who we are is vital to our communication skills. In the public stereotypes of archaeologists, we are myopic, dedicated to the quest for the past. No small number of archaeologists see themselves as Indiana Jones types: adventurous, attending to social convention only as necessary to pay the bills, something of a loner, and dedicated more than anything to protection of the past. Some of this brashness and insensitivity translates into our work, with one archaeologist (Mason 1997) even going so far as to declare that our job is to challenge peoples' oral traditions!

Most archaeologists are not so insensitive, but our approaches often alienate as much as educate. We are not a discipline that has normally valued writing for the public; in fact, in academia doing so has often been frowned upon by promotion and tenure committees. We are also a field that is vastly more critical of the work of peers than are scholars in many other fields, and it does not serve us well with our audiences. Our public bloodlettings more often make us appear to be jealous and petty. In terms of communicating with our publics and sometimes even our colleagues, we seem not to care whether our audiences understand us at all. Some seem to have a "let them eat cake" attitude: If they can't understand my terminology and my syntax, they are nothing but uneducated louts, so screw 'em!

If you are entering the field of archaeology or are a relatively new professional, some good advice suggests that you can be both a decent human being *and* a good archaeologist. In no way can this book change your basic attitudes, but perhaps it can make you think differently about the way you communicate with both colleagues and various archaeological publics. Nowhere is our insensitivity more apparent than in our use of jargon, so let's start there.

JARGON

Some years ago, I got into a discussion with a historian colleague, both of us Plains specialists, about why American Indians—and, for that matter, the general public—didn't pay much attention to archaeologists. He proposed a couple of possibilities, both on target. He maintained that ordinary people, including Indians, pretty much wanted to know about tribes with familiar names, and he asked why we archaeologists were so reluctant to assign tribal names to prehistoric people. I pointed out that population movement and culture histories were rather more complex than simply assigning tribal names, most of those designated by white people, anyway. After all, as a profession we had countless arguments about taxonomy. It was no small feat to document the culture history of any group archaeologically, and we didn't want to fall victim to the simplistic schemes that some historians often proposed. Then he leveled an accusation: "How the hell is someone supposed to understand the subtleties of what the Terminal variant of the Initial Middle Missouri phase means, anyway?"

He had a good point. We archaeologists do love our jargon. Being raised as a processual archaeologist in the late 1960s and early 1970s, I recall the jargon flowing freely. There were new paradigms galore, and terms like *deviation amplification* brought an intellectual orgasm. A student had to be up on the latest usage to be "with it." The analytical archaeology course I took in 1971 was a veritable jargon orgy!

Jargon is not just made up, empty, meaningless words. It is specialized language and can promote extremely efficient communication if everyone involved knows it. However, jargon can also be empty and meaningless, not to mention boring, to someone who doesn't know the code. The problem for archaeology is that when we use jargon, we can rarely be assured that even our colleagues know what it means, let alone the nonspecialist. It's fine to talk Terminal Middle Missouri variant to a colleague who is also a specialist in Plains Village cultures of the northern Plains, but one might want to avoid doing so to a colleague who might specialize in the Plains Village cultures of the southern Plains. Certainly you wouldn't want to use it with an avocational archaeologist. You would probably be better off saying "ancestral Mandan" so she at least has an inkling of what you are talking about, in spite of the risk of possible misunderstandings on technical issues about whether Terminal Middle Missouri might have associations with other Siouan-speaking groups.

The point here is simple: Let the jargon match the audience. Jargon is fine so long as it has relatively wide acceptance. Use jargon carefully, usually only with those groups you are relatively certain know the meanings. Writing about Terminal Middle Missouri variant is fine for *Plains Anthropologist*, a professional journal, but it wasn't so good for my *Peoples of Prehistoric South Dakota*, a popular book on South

Dakota archaeology. If using jargon is crucial to accuracy, then it might be important to contextualize it by taking the time to explain what it means. One need not write down to an audience, but one should certainly respect the limitations of their knowledge and training and give them the opportunity to understand. The real problem for many of us is that we are so used to our jargon, we don't even really recognize that it is jargon. We use *projectile point* so often we rarely realize that most people use the more specific *arrowhead* or *spearhead* (even though they might be wrong about the kind of projectile point it is!).

Jargon is especially difficult in CRM reports because the audience is not always clear. Colleagues who review your report, and hopefully the archaeologists who work for the agency for which the report is being done, will at least have some clue about the jargon. CRM reports do have other audiences, including contract managers, planners, and other cultural heritage administrators, who haven't a clue about the jargon. Along with protecting site-sensitive information, aversion to our jargon is one reason that many agencies demand public versions of many CRM reports.

Jargon is only one element in working with audiences. So many other issues about how we present the past stem from who we think comprises our audience. The media we choose to communicate with them are also crucial, which is the subject of the next chapter.

3

 CHOOSING THE RIGHT MEDIUM

With so many media available today, from standard print sources to a range of new electronic media, how do you choose those that are best for presenting your work? The answers are not as simple as one might think. For those working in the academic sphere, most still treasure the printed media of books and journals. CRM specialists may have to consider publication in multiple ways given stipulations of a project's scope of work. Independent research projects may allow substantial freedom to choose any medium you wish. However, additional complications may be related to intended audiences.

Certainly, professional books, journals, and CRM reports are not the best way to reach a general audience or perhaps even a professional audience who does not specialize in your area of interest but who may benefit by knowing something of your work. Given increased efforts at public outreach, many agency CRM managers discovered a long time ago that public versions of reports were a good idea, making preparation of such documents part of scopes of work. Even with reports prepared at more than one level, delivery of the documents to the intended audiences can be a problem. Books, journals, and even glossy public reports are costly to produce, and purchasing them is no small matter for many of us, let alone for a general public with a less than fanatic interest in archaeology.

Essentially, you need to ask the following questions in deciding on a medium:

1. Who is my intended audience?
2. What are my contractual or other obligations to these audiences?

3. What kind of budget do I have to prepare my work?
4. Given these factors, what media are available to me?
5. What will it cost to distribute my work to the intended audiences?

Let's look briefly at each of these questions.

WHO IS MY INTENDED AUDIENCE?

Chapter 2 provided a discussion of audiences that might have led you to think that audience is easy to determine. If so, you are probably thinking too narrowly. Avocational archaeologists, for example, often read articles written for state archaeological journals. Professional colleagues might also use your World Wide Web site developed for a lay audience to prepare lectures for their introductory classes. Consider a range of possibilities when you prepare materials. This doesn't mean that you necessarily have to "dumb down" presentations or that you have to continually worry about what colleagues might think. What it does mean is that with relatively little planning and effort, you should be able to provide satisfactory materials for several audiences at once.

WHAT ARE MY CONTRACTUAL OR OTHER OBLIGATIONS TO THESE AUDIENCES?

You may have contractual obligations that instruct you to gear your presentations toward particular audiences. If you are working on a CRM project, check the scope of work carefully to see who intended audiences will be. If it is just for a state or federal agency CRM specialist, you may only need an administrative report, one that can be loaded with CRM jargon for efficient communication aimed at best protecting the resource. You and the agency manager both know what a Phase I Reconnaissance Survey is. If the scope says the report will be sent out for review, however, your problem is more complex. Is it a report to be reviewed by other CRM agencies, or are professional specialist colleagues with intimate knowledge of an area also to be reviewers? If the latter, you may need to provide more detailed information on theory and culture history than the CRM manager might find understandable, so you'll need to find a middle ground or provide adequate, clear explanation of jargon in the text. Many larger CRM projects now require as part of the scope of work that the contractor prepare a shorter version of the project's findings for the general public.

You may thus find yourself having to prepare a multilevel report, but don't assume that you can just abstract the longer report into the shorter report. Jargon is jargon, and a nonprofessional audience still might not understand it, nor will they likely care about your justification for your sampling method or detailed descriptions of each flake found by your surveyors. Regular contact with your contracting officer might help you find an appropriate level for each report.

For non-CRM reports, you will be writing for a specific audience from the start. If you suspect multilevel audience concerns might apply, and even though you won't have contractual obligations for multiple-level reporting, you might discuss the issues with your editor. If you can provide for different audiences, you will likely increase the size of your audiences.

WHAT KIND OF BUDGET DO I HAVE TO PREPARE MY WORK?

Of course, this question is one you should have asked before you took on a project! If you are doing a CRM report, there may be particular requirements for distribution of the report. For example, the United States National Park Service has recently started requiring that contractors prepare both a hard copy of the report and also an electronic copy in a .pdf format (portable document file) for easy insertion on the World Wide Web or on a CD-ROM. Although the Adobe Acrobat software itself is inexpensive, there will be some time, and possibly substantial labor costs for converting your report to .pdf files. When you prepare a cost proposal or bid for a contract, you might wish to factor in some of these cost elements.

Your manuscripts, reports, or other projects may require lots of detailed graphics. Web and CD-ROM presentations may also require skill in web markup, design, or even instructional design to be effective for an intended audience. If you are like most archaeologists, you probably aren't trained as a graphic artist or design specialist, let alone a computer programmer or education specialist. You may need to hire additional staff or outsource some of the work. Hiring work done by others adds to your costs.

A CAUTION

Everyone wants to do work of the highest quality, although we sometimes find it less than practical to do so due to the many constraints of time, personnel, budget, and, frankly, our own (lack of?) talent and that of our staff. Most of us have been trained to consider what we do to be part of a scientific process of archaeology and hope to add something, however small, to the culture history or key research topics of the areas in which we work. This often motivates us to do more than is necessary for what the people paying the bills really need.

This point is especially true for small CRM projects. Why prepare a ten-page report when an agency will allow a letter report? More than one state historical preservation review and compliance officer have received lengthy reports with "boilerplate" culture histories and major methodological descriptions that report no sites and contain only a few paragraphs about survey methods. Your time and that of your staff is valuable. Why waste it trying to do "science" when what the entire agency wants is a report to help its staff manage the cultural resources for which they are responsible?

GIVEN THESE FACTORS, WHAT MEDIA ARE AVAILABLE TO ME?

This is not usually a tough call. Most of us will probably fall back on the standard hard-copy paper report, but given the rapidly increasing number of options, perhaps we should be more selective. If we need only prepare a letter report or a report of a few pages, paper is just fine. If we have to prepare a report of some length, with the bulk of it done on a word processor, then why not consider publishing it in some electronic format, if the contracting agency is willing or if the audience is appropriate? The savings can be substantial, and the amount of included material provided to readers can be expanded.

WHAT WILL IT COST TO DISTRIBUTE MY WORK TO THE INTENDED AUDIENCES?

This may not always be your problem, but it may be that of the agency or publisher. Its staff will also be thinking about how to best present materials to a particular audience. Someone has to think about it, so it might be best if you think of it as you prepare a report, a paper, or a book. It may make the difference in getting published!

Lots of questions regarding the report seem to appear almost immediately. Should you include photographs? Would color illustrations be useful? What sort of figures do you need, how many of them, and how big? Do you have lots of tabular data that you would like to include but that only a few readers might find useful? If you can plan ahead a bit while you prepare a document, you'll be better off in the long run when it comes to producing the final product.

CONCLUSION

When it comes to all the questions in chapters 3 and 4 about audience and media, one thing becomes clear very quickly: Presenting the past is complicated! One shouldn't think that it is a matter of just sitting down and writing. Differing audiences require you to think about the ways in which you can present the past. Differing media require different kinds of skills. Most archaeologists haven't thought much about the skills they need to present the past or how to go about acquiring them. The next chapter aims to remedy that situation.

4

DEVELOPING NEEDED SKILLS AND TOOLS

You wouldn't go to the field without a reasonably well-developed research design to guide your survey or excavations, and you certainly couldn't do the work without the right tools. The same should apply to presenting the past. You might develop a strategy for preparing manuscripts, drawings, or photographs whether you are doing a CRM report, a book, or an article.

BASIC WRITING SKILLS

Just as we don't like to have untrained people working in the field or lab, we should not assume that it's okay to have untrained people preparing reports. During the many years that I ran a CRM operation for the University of South Dakota, I had the opportunity to read the many reports prepared by our lab staff. Some were excellent, but many had to be rewritten before they went out. Bright people wrote most of them, but they obviously didn't have writing skills. These days, managers in the business world often like to complain that fresh college graduates come to them without basic communication skills, and I'm afraid to admit that they are mostly right. Usually, on-the-job training can help people overcome the problem, but it takes close supervision, something that may be a luxury in a small CRM operation.

When colleagues have called me for references for colleagues or former students who are seeking employment with some CRM firm, one of the most commonly asked questions has been either "Can they write?" or "Can you get reports out of them?" For CRM firms, this is no small matter. Projects are done to deadlines, and if the project staff can't produce the report, people might not get paid, and the next contract might be impossible to get.

If you are hiring new people, don't hesitate to ask them for writing samples. If they can't produce one, or they give you one that's not well written, don't hire them. If you have staff who write poorly and you'd like to keep them, you can provide training. If, heaven forbid, you are yourself not so good at writing, you may wish to take some training. This book is not meant to be a writing handbook; thousands of "how to write" books are available. However, a few concepts might help you understand some of the problems of writing and get you thinking about developing and shaping your own or some staff member's basic writing skills.

WRITING IS A LINEAR MEDIUM MADE UP OF CIRCULAR THINKING

When we put words on paper, we tend to think of the process in terms of X leading to Y leading to Z, a nice straight line sequence. Even our thinking as archaeologists is posed in this way in terms of time where culture X came before culture Y and culture Z. The problem is that even our analyses of archaeological cultures don't proceed that way. They just end up that way on a culture history chart or in our article about a site. The actual process is more meandering. We sort and measure sherds hoping to do a ceramic seriation, we attempt to correlate certain styles with certain strata to give us a sequence, and so forth. In the end, we impose a kind of linearity on our materials. The process is difficult, without question!

Writing is also like that, and we'd be better off if we just recognized this fact from the start. I've had more problems with introductions than I care to think about. Even in this book, as I write this chapter, I've only begun to think about writing the introduction! I'm also certain that it will be rewritten about five times before I actually send it in. I've also had more students fail to submit papers because they couldn't get past the introduction. I've also written the sections on preparing abstracts, giving conference papers, and dealing with the media before I tackled this section.

Few of us are capable of enough organizational skill to just sit down and write something from beginning to end. We don't think that way, so why should we force ourselves to write that way? We think in jumbled ways. We go over and over things in our heads. We try to puzzle out things. There's nothing wrong with writing parts of a book, paper, or anything else "out of order." Ultimately these things do need to be put in a linear sequence. Readers can't follow the jumble in our heads. So how do you get there?

OUTLINES HELP IMPOSE WRITING'S LINEAR STRUCTURE

Writing an outline is something most of us were taught in elementary school, but with the press of writing papers against deadlines, most of us quickly forget how valuable they actually are. Outlines are really nothing but an overview of where you intend to go with your writing. They need not be cast in stone and, in fact, should be malleable as "great thoughts" surface about what you are writing.

For some kinds of books, though, outlines must be detailed and essentially allow little deviation. A colleague and I worked on a book for a publisher who demanded a detailed outline ahead of time so his design staff could get busy with layout. We had to think in terms of two-page "spreads" that would have 600 words, with a box that would have 150 words. This was tough, but when it came time to actually write, it was unbelievably easy. In fact, the outline took longer than the writing, the former about three months and the latter only a month!

Many people actually do an outline in their heads, so why not put it on paper? Doing so allows you to write on various parts at different times. In this way, you'll see the writing as connected, but you won't be locked into linear writing. An added benefit on large projects is that outlines allow you to break the project into pieces of manageable size so you don't feel overwhelmed.

TELL 'EM WHAT YOU'RE GOING TO TELL 'EM, TELL 'EM, AND TELL 'EM WHAT YOU TOLD 'EM

In the U.S. Air Force, we were taught this adage about being direct and concise, in both writing and speaking, especially when we were presenting information to higher-ranking officers who supposedly had little time. The adage is a lesson in linearity, but it also makes a point about structure and reinforcement of points as you move through a work. In essence, it is the old writing structure about introduction, body, and conclusion, which you might have learned in your first composition classes. The introduction contains your primary theses and statements about how you will demonstrate your contentions. The body contains data, examples, and thinking about both, but organized in a logical and replicable fashion. Your conclusion contains the assessment of your data and argumentation, as well inferences about it.

In classes I usually tell students how to do well on my essay exams or papers. I liken the writing process to that of sands in an hourglass. At the top of the hourglass, the glass is wide and there is a clutter of ideas. You need to tell the reader generally about the body of information you have and how you are going to organize it. As the sand passes through the constriction, it flows through a grain or two at a time. This is the detailed presentation of data and examples, with the constriction being the logic you impose on it. These data and examples collect in the bottom of the hourglass, but they are hopefully now in a slightly more ordered state than they were. This more organized collection is your conclusion, where you tell the reader what it all means.

I tell students that this structure also should apply to each unit, chapter, or paragraph in the work. For the latter, one uses the general topic sentence to start a paragraph, followed by the body of the paragraph, which contains data and logic, and the transition sentence, which leads the reader to the next topic sentence. Certainly, other analogies might suffice and the approach may not work for all forms of writing, but after you've read a few student essays, you understand how few people really understand the linear structure of writing. In archaeology, you can write using a stream of consciousness, but you'll probably get the report sent back to you by your professor, boss, or the contracting agency!

UNDERSTAND THAT YOUR WORDS ARE NOT ALL THAT PRECIOUS

Sportswriter Red Smith commented more or less, "Writing is easy. You sit down at the typewriter and open a vein." After you've slaved away for hours, days, or months on a manuscript, it's really tough to have somebody critique your work. If you take writing seriously, you put some of your lifeblood into it, so every word seems to be one of those drops of blood, but you know that losing a few drops won't kill you. If you give it some serious thought, you will recognize that most of what you write as a professional archaeologist is not poetry, in which well-chosen words may actually be precious. Your writing can almost become formulaic or "boilerplate" in the CRM world, where you need to crank out reports relatively quickly. Even in your other work, your quest is usually for easily understood, rapidly written prose. As one who has edited several books and professional journals, I can tell you straightforwardly that nothing is more of a pain than an author who thinks his or her words are "golden." (More on working with editors later.) You'll write more rapidly, be a more likable person to editors, and generally be a happier soul if you understand that letting others see and comment on your work can improve it.

THE MORE YOU WRITE, THE BETTER YOU GET

Writing is like anything else. The more you practice, the better you get. If you start an exercise program, your muscles sometimes hurt if you aren't used to it. Writing is the same way. If you haven't written much, it's tough at the beginning but gets easier.

Writers tend to develop various strategies that work for them. Some insist that you have to write some every day, but as with exercise, that takes great discipline, perhaps even obsession. At the same time, if you can write a page or two a day, you've got a solid book at the end of each and every year.

Most people will never be that disciplined. If you are like some, you may "write" every day, though not always on paper. You may be one to mull over a subject in your head, then "download" it in nearly finished form to your word processor. Some like to worry about word choice from the beginning, slaving like Flaubert to find *le mot juste.* Others are more concerned with content and meaning, spewing a James Joyce–like stream of consciousness, with any wordsmithing saved for the end.

You need to develop your own strategies for writing. If you haven't thought about it much, look at how you tend to go about things and what works for you. However, don't make excuses or lie to yourself about your real approach. Once you've got a strategy figured out, stick to it, and practice, practice, practice.

READ LOTS, BUT PAY ATTENTION TO THE WRITING, NOT JUST THE CONTENT

You really can't be a good writer unless you pay attention to good writing. You can learn a great deal by reading others. Certainly, archaeologists have a style. One simple example is our use of the passive voice. We accept passive voice more than most other fields because it's really difficult to know who acted on what in the past in order to allow the active voice. Mostly, we just don't pay attention. (If you don't know what I'm talking about here, it's the difference between the following sentences: "The excavation grid was laid out by the crew" [passive] versus "The crew laid out the excavation grid" [active].) At the same time, you also see approaches you like and don't like, so you can model your approach to what you like.

FIND ONE OR TWO GOOD WRITING REFERENCES AND USE THEM

It is really important that you have a basic writing book by your desk or an electronic version on your computer and use it. If your style is more conservative, this might be a book such as Strunk and White's *The Elements of Style*, from Allyn and Bacon (2000). If you are younger and more in tune with the information age, you might like Verve Press's (1999) *Adios, Strunk and White: A Handbook for the New Academic Essay* by Gary and Glynis Hoffman. Another favorite is *Line by Line: How to Improve Your Own Writing* by Claire Kehrwald Cook, published by Houghton Mifflin (1986) for the Modern Language Association. Its strength is that the author has been a copyeditor and provides techniques used by editors. She gives insights into how editors think about text when they work over a manuscript. The standard for all writers, however, is *The Chicago Manual of Style*, used by everyone in the publishing process. Its primary strength comes from its currency. Constant revision keeps it up-to-date, and recent editions have emphasized the process of publishing as much as the elements of writing. Which book you have is probably not all that important; you just need to have some basic writing guides at your disposal.

Besides having these guides, having access to a good dictionary, thesaurus, and other basic writing tools should go without saying, but oddly enough, most people don't have them nearby. Good, inexpensive dictionaries and other reference tools are available for your computer. Some word processors have simple tools built in, where all you need to do is to highlight a word and click on the tool(s). There are also many such tools available on line. *Your Dictionary* (www.yourdictionary.com/) is one good example, providing a wide range of English and other language tools, but there are many others. There's not much excuse for not having access to these resources.

SOME FINAL POINTS ABOUT WRITING BASICS

You can follow all the advice offered thus far. You can buy books galore on writing and study them in depth. You can fantasize about writing all you like. What it comes down to is sitting your rear end in a chair, putting your fingers on the keyboard, and grinding away. That's the single hardest part. Even after thirty years of writing I still have to force myself into the chair, and frankly, it doesn't get all that much easier. However, no matter what you may think about the prose in this book, after thirty years, the writing *has* gotten better!

BEYOND THE BASICS OF WRITING

Assuming you have some level of mastery over basic writing and some level of self-discipline about doing it, you can work toward acquiring additional tools. As presented in the following paragraphs, they don't necessarily come with any priority but are tied to the concept of making writing easier and you more capable of providing a product, whether it be a paper for a graduate seminar, a full-blown CRM report, or a scholarly monograph.

STYLES AND HOW TO DEAL WITH THEM

Figuring out writing styles is one of the most difficult elements in writing, especially when you have to write for a wide range of audiences. As I'm writing this, I'm glancing over at a copy of *Dig* magazine for kids. I'm contemplating writing a piece on "fringe" archaeology that one of the contributing editors asked me to think about. Frankly, the task is daunting at best. Writing for kids can be a bear when you have been writing academic archaeology for thirty years. We archaeologists have our own style, with its own jargon, sentence structure, and linear presentation, and I have to wonder whether I can do it.

Even in considering the style of this series and volume, the editors and publisher had several discussions about what we could and couldn't do. We didn't want lots of in-text citations or footnotes common to academic writing because they tend to disrupt the flow of text for a reader. We wanted more of a textbook style, but even there we had concerns. We wanted to keep the text "light," with relatively little jargon and few overly complex sentences. To do this, we needed to keep things more conversational in tone, so we allowed authors to use contractions and other writing styles usually anathema to academic writing, such as using arcane words such as *anathema* and *arcane*.

So, how can you figure out what style is for what audience? The first thing to do is to read widely within archaeology to get an idea of the range of styles that we use. If you can assess a target audience, you might be able to figure out what the style might be. If it's for a popular audience, vocabulary and sentence structures should be less complex. Jargon should be fully explained or absent. For more educated lay audiences, sentence structures can be complex, as can vocabulary, but jargon should still be minimized. For professional audiences, in which scholars know the jargon and are used to the style, you can write for that audience, but the style should not be convoluted or the prose turgid.

ARCHAEOLOGICAL STYLES AND HIDDEN AUDIENCES

Once you've figured out what style is for what audience, you then need to craft the prose for that group. Mitch Allen (2002) has taken a close look at what he calls archaeology's "hidden audience"—nonspecialists—and how to write for them in particular. He provides an analysis of who they are and gives ten tips for writing for them. Of course, you must also write for professional colleagues, so let's take look at how this can play out using some examples from my own writing (I choose them not because I think they are particularly good, but so that I don't have to pick on anyone else!). I've chosen selections from writings about the Crow Creek massacre and the associated issue of repatriation, mostly because I've done lots of pieces on each for a range of audiences.

Let's start with a recent piece for an educated audience, but not just professional colleagues (Zimmerman 2001:169). In considering my audience, I understood from the editor that readers would be educated, concerned with human rights issues, and at least moderately aware of repatriation debates. Here is part of the second paragraph:

> But do archaeologists export the data and move the creative process and their results away from Native American nations? The answer is unequivocally yes. American Archaeology is an edifice of scientific colonialism, and this has crippled its relationships with Native Americans. The crucible of the repatriation and reburial issues has made it painfully

clear that archaeological interactions with Indians often have been inept and torturous. Many Native Americans go so far as to call archaeology irrelevant or inaccurate.

Notice that the sentence structure is somewhat complex, but with only one compound sentence, and there are lots of difficult words (e.g., *edifice, crucible, inept, torturous*). There is one concept, scientific colonialism, that is jargon, which I actually define in the first sentence of the piece.

Work for a fully professional audience of archaeologists can be more data-dense, as in this paragraph taken from an article about the Crow Creek massacre for *Plains Anthropologist*, a professional journal (Zimmerman and Bradley 1993:217). A few nonspecialists might read it, but there was no expectation of that. Midway through the piece is a discussion of malnutrition in the remains:

> In preliminary evaluation of the skeletal materials, investigators found numerous transverse lines in radiographs of long bones. Examination also revealed evidence suggesting iron deficiency anemia in 28 skulls, 18 with orbital cribra, four with orbital cribra associated with other skull lesions, and six with porotic hyperostisis. Both localized and generalized periostial reactions were very prevalent in the Crow Creek bones. Subsequent investigations have uncovered additional supporting evidence indicating repetitious and prolonged malnutrition in many Crow Creek Skeletons.

Ouch! This paragraph is actually one that requires not only archaeology jargon but also knowledge of osteology and paleopathology. Do you know what a periostial reaction is? These terms never get defined in the text. Sentence structure is relatively complex, with several clauses, and the paragraph is data-dense.

Let's now look at a paragraph from my *Peoples of Prehistoric South Dakota* geared toward an audience of nonspecialists. Certainly, some colleagues would use the book, but South Dakota citizens were the target audience. They would range from junior high school students through adults. The paragraph again describes Crow Creek (Zimmerman 1985:51):

> Archaeologists know from skeletons found at the site that a pattern of warfare had been going on for some time. At least two individuals had been scalped earlier and had survived, only to be killed during the Crow Creek massacre. Others had been wounded earlier by arrows, the points embedded in bone, which had grown over them.

This paragraph has some complexity, with several clauses and one compound sentence, but words are relatively short, with no real jargon. There is one instance of passive voice ("Others had been . . ."), which I would now change. Sentence length is longer than one might write for children, and vocabulary is more complex.

I wrote the following paragraph for a Crow Creek Massacre website (www.usd.edu/anth/crow/ccwhat.html) specifically aimed at middle school children:

> Some archaeologists believe that the attack was carried out by the Middle Missouri villagers who came down from the north. They might have been unhappy that the Initial Coalescent people had moved into the area and had taken their land. Other archaeologists do not believe this is a good explanation. These scientists believe that the cause had to do with the environment and overpopulation.

The vocabulary is more limited and sentence structure a bit simpler. I notice a pesky passive voice, which I would now change. The content is more emotional, from the point of view of both the reasons for the massacre and the difference of opinion among the archaeologists. Children are probably the most difficult to write for because their abilities change so quickly. For children, ways to present the past need to be more action oriented and emotional.

What do kids like to read about archaeology? To some degree, they like to read about other kids. In looking at each piece in *Dig*, the first thing I noticed was that all but two of the articles and many of the news items started with a question within the first line or two. I suppose this approach is to get the child thinking about the subject, but it also helps set a kind of imaginary stage. Here's an example:

> About 20,000–30,000 years ago, an 8- to 10-year-old boy skidded barefoot through a muddy cave in what is now southern France. Think that kid would get a kick out of knowing that his tootsie marks would become the oldest footprints ever found in Europe?

You should notice that the first sentence sets a temporal and spatial stage, but, more important, it sets the action. The question is a hook, drawing the child into the scene. You might also notice that the tone is conversational and that the question is not even a proper sentence.

Many of you might scoff at such approaches if you found them in a student's paper or a colleague's report, but consider that the approach is successful. *Dig*'s subscription base is growing dramatically, with an even higher readership, and questions e-mailed to "Dr. Dig" are surprisingly numerous and sophisticated.

Finally, let's look briefly at fiction with a paragraph from my only published short story (Zimmerman 1986), "Redwing," a pair of vignettes, one set in the past and one in the present, linked by a skeleton and a bird:

> He seldom thought about the people represented by the village debris. He couldn't know their individual lives, only the general patterns of their daily existence. When he worked with burials, however, they made it more personal. Knowing that he was working on a young female caused him to see Sarah. He still didn't understand why she had to die. She was only 37.

The style is looser, close to that for children's writing, with relatively short sentences. The paragraph actually contains an important theoretical idea about how archaeologists see individuals, but in the emotional context of Sarah's death. Fiction allows a writer to push the edges of grammar a bit, with sentence structure that may not be standard. You can play with point of view in ways not available to you in nonfiction, and active voice is crucial. In fiction, a style is more difficult to pin down because it is so open and variable.

For the most part, archaeology students learn style through osmosis. Professors rarely teach anything about it, even if a department happens to have a writing course. In a way, that's too bad, because we would be much better communicators if we did. The problem with hoping students will learn by absorbing what they read is that much of what students, especially graduate students, read is the cutting-edge material in a profession. Obviously, they need to do that, but cutting-edge materials are often the most logically complex and jargon-laden prose in a profession. Theory is supposed to be simple, but explaining theory usually isn't. Because their professors praise their students' supposed understanding of complex articles on theory, students read more and more of it, mouthing the jargon but sometimes not really understanding it. We often use it to impress each other rather than to communicate. In the end, very impressed people can be talking away, not really understanding each other! The same is true of our writing.

You may be tempted to say that you shouldn't have to worry about whether the masses can understand your prose. Remember, however, that you've probably often thought of the contract manager for some CRM project as having the intelligence of a charcoal sample. Do you really want your report rejected because the stupid bureaucrat can't understand what you've written? Just tone it down. Table 4.1 summarizes some tips for keeping your writing clean and simple, and sidebar 4.1 describes a useful tool for helping in that regard: readability indexes.

DEALING WITH REFERENCES

As if style wasn't enough of a problem, writing has a number of technical aspects to complicate matters. If you are reading this book, you have already probably written at least a few papers and know some of the problems. References seem to be a problem for lots of writers. The need for them is fundamentally simple: Readers need to know how you arrived at your conclusions. All scholarship is not done in a vacuum but is cumulative, built on the work of others.

Our readers need to be able to connect what we've concluded to the work of others, the data we've used, and what our work implies. The reader also has a right to know who provided what elements of your thinking. They might like to know whether you actually quoted or interpreted another scholar correctly. You might have taken some

---

Table 4.1. Tips to Help Simplify Your Writing

1. Figure out who your audience is.
2. Write shorter sentences by eliminating compound sentences (you know, the ones with conjunctions).
3. Try eliminating clauses.
4. Count multiple-syllable words, which are often more abstract (think jargon here).
5. Use shorter words wherever possible, lowering the average number of syllables per word.
6. Don't be afraid to write in first person.
7. Use active voice wherever possible.
8. Use anecdotes and stories to raise the emotional content.
9. Every so often, calculate a readability index to see whether your writing meets what you think the appropriate reading level is for your audience. If it doesn't, then rewrite.
10. Read the work aloud. Normally, people don't speak in as complicated a way as they write. If the prose sounds complicated, it probably is.

4.1. READABILITY INDEXES

Can you learn to write at several different levels and really know what you are doing? One approach is to use readability indexes. These provide a grade-level estimate of skills required to understand written material. Although there are on-going debates about what this really means, the tools can still be used to estimate relative difficulty of materials for readers.
Most indexes tend to:

- count the number of words in a sentence;
- count the words with three or more syllables;
- look at prepositions, such as *of, from, with,* and *by,* which tend to make sentences too long and destroy sentence rhythm; and
- look at "lazy words" such as *and, it, this,* and *there* or "personal" words or sentences including pronouns.

This approach does provide subjectivity. If you want more information, look at Dr. Jay's *Power Writing Home Page* (www.csun.edu/~vcecn006/read1.htm), which provides an excellent summary of many such tools.
Do readability indexes work? They can help you learn basic skills, but you can't use them to check everything. You are better off learning the problem areas of writing that add complexity and teaching yourself different styles of writing.

idea out of context or misunderstood what another author wrote. Much of this has to do with the idea that science is supposed to be replicable, so being able to follow the reasoning of another scholar is important. Most writers know this, and there really is no reason to fight against it, as I've seen many students do.

DO YOU REALLY NEED THAT CITATION?

One of the biggest debates in writing is whether to use citations or at what level you should cite your sources. Avocational archaeologists often hate citations, as do nonacademics in general. Whether super-scripted numbers for footnotes or in-text citations, they certainly disrupt the flow of text for the reader. Certainly, if one is doing academic writing for colleagues, citation is imperative! However, most of us who've written for a long time tend to get warped a bit in graduate school. As professors read our papers, the query "Source?" commonly appeared in the margin or next to some idea. In addition, as students learn the process of academic writing, they learn citation overkill, where they string together several citations about one general idea. One doesn't have to read much to see this in archaeological writing. If an idea is common knowledge, you may not need to cite another source at all. (Check out sidebar 4.2 for a quick discussion of copyrights and plagiarism, which are another big reason why we need to mess with references in the first place.)

An important consideration is the intended audience. For popular works, avoid lots of citations. Audiences neither like nor need them. They accept your reasoning as an authority (although most of us would advise them not to) or the argumentation itself (the wiser approach). When writing for young people, avoid citations altogether. A better approach for anything popular is to have a section of sources and suggested readings, kept as brief as possible. Even for some professional publications, lots of citations may be unnecessary. Textbooks are an example, on the border between popular and professional. You'll

4.2.   PLAGIARISM AND COPYRIGHT

Plagiarism is using the ideas or words of others without giving them credit. Plagiarism has become more common, especially with the World Wide Web and other digital media providing easy means of finding and directly copying text from published works. Many students claim not to know that plagiarism is wrong, and several scholars have blamed careless research for not taking notes that some words are direct quotes.

Paraphrasing the work of others is generally okay, but the idea should be attributed to them with a citation. A good rule of thumb is "When in doubt, cite!" Some kinds of popular writing don't allow citation in the text, so be certain to paraphrase and then to list the work in your sources or acknowledgments.

Copyright is legal ownership of words, ideas, images, and sounds. Use requires permission. Generally academic works allow more flexibility than popular works. Attributed quotations of several lines are considered "fair use," but seek permission for use of very long quotations, especially if there are lots of them. (This includes illustrations or music.) Generally you seek permission from the holder of the copyright. This may be the publisher or author, and it may involve a fee for use or a particular credit line they would like you to use. The work usually lists the holder of copyright. The general rule: When in doubt, ask permission!

see that publishers use different approaches to them. In this series, the series editors and the publisher made a conscious decision to keep citations to a minimum. We rely instead on suggested readings, largely because The Archaeologist's Toolkit books are like textbooks or handbooks, not academic treatises.

The real reason references upset writers is that their research is poorly organized. You've often been in a hurry doing research, with a class or contract report deadline looming. The written materials you've found excite you. The source you've got is excellent, and you are scribbling notes like crazy. In the rush, you don't note the page number of the source, or the volume number, or the first names of the editor. When it comes time to put in the reference, you simply don't have the unrecorded element in your notes. Nothing—that's right, *nothing*—is more frustrating than to be held up by such piddling details! If you've got the source in your own personal library, this might not seem like a big deal. However, a trek to the university library is far less fun, and you've got a special headache if the volume you just took back there three days ago was one that took weeks for your interlibrary loan librarian to track down!

If you can't have a source right in front of you when you write, which is usually the case on a large project, you may need a system to help you keep careful track of sources and information. I use an approach that can be useful, but I assure you that I preach it far better than I practice it!

Normally, as I read something that I am not using immediately for a writing project, I have a notebook or computer with me. The first element that I put on a page is an absolutely complete bibliographic citation including the book's ISBN and library call number in the place I found it. As I'll get to soon, I know from experience that several different bibliographic styles are favored by archaeologists and other anthropologists, so I try to cover all the bases, everything from publisher location to full author names exactly as they are on the copyright or title page. I start through the work, taking notes along the way. As I take a note, I leave space in the left-hand margin for the page number from which I take an idea or about which I write a comment. These are normally paraphrases or snippets of the text. If I think a quotation is cool, I copy it down, with the page number in the left-hand margin. I put quotation marks around the text! Then I double-check the quotation to see that I have it down correctly, even to the capitalization and punctuation. This step is important: If you don't get it down correctly, you can do substantial damage to your own work, let alone misrepresent the work of someone else. Besides, tracking down a quotation later is often more difficult than getting publication information on a source.

As I have time to digest the work, I often think about how it connects to my own projects (common), or I'll come up with some brilliant, synthetic thoughts of my own (rare). For both, I put "P.N." in the margin for "Personal Note" to let myself know later that these are my thoughts about the work. I proceed through the book or article this way, often generating many pages of notes (see table 4.2 for a sample page).

I hear students and colleagues talk about taking marginal notes in books, even to the point of having strata of notes on second or third readings. Others highlight key elements with markers. These approaches assume that you own the volume—God forbid, and shame on you, that you do this in a library copy! The problem with both approaches is that you have to go back to the original to get material you need. Besides, writing notes helps you remember the material better.

What note taking allows is full bibliographic control of your research. This approach is really no different from what you were prob-

---

Table 4.2.   Sample Notebook Page for Bibliographic and Research Control

Source: Feder, Kenneth L.
   2002 *Frauds, Myths, and Mysteries: Science and Pseudoscience in Archaeology*. McGraw-Hill Mayfield, Boston. 4th edition.
   ISBN: 0-7674-2722-X, UI Library Call Number: CC140.F43.2001

p. 2   Survey among tv viewers showed 25% believe in fortune telling, 12% in astrology, 22% in clairvoyance, 3% in fortune cookies.

P.N.   This corresponds highly with the numbers in the "gullibility" index I give my Lost Tribes, etc., class.

p. 4   Feder notes that his own college classes show beliefs similar to the public; see his charts on p. 5.

p. 6   "'Science,' after all, is merely a process of understanding the world around us through the application of logical thought."

P.N.   . . . is science perfect? "Of course not."
   Science has rejected seemingly outrageous claims (plate tectonics) only to have them proved right.

ably taught about using 3 × 5–inch index cards for taking notes and organizing research. Computers have changed all that, of course. I still like to have a notebook for note taking, but I do often take my laptop to the library for research. I still take notes in more or less the same way, but in a database or in my word processor. The query functions of most database programs and find functions of a word processor allow fast searching for terms or strings of text. There are also stand-alone text analysis programs to do this for you. You can easily search your whole database for related terms or concepts. Mostly, they allow you to get things organized and keep track of tons of materials easily, even over a whole career.

BUILDING A PERSONAL OR COMPANY ANNOTATED BIBLIOGRAPHY

By the time you hit graduate school, you know that you have read and will continue to read books, monographs, CRM reports, and articles as a regular part of your scholarship and pleasure. If I could give only one piece of advice to graduate students or young professional archaeologists, I would suggest that you start as soon as possible to build a lifetime annotated bibliography of all you read. I certainly wish that I had done so. As adept as you might be at remembering what you read, you will come to a point at which you tell yourself, "Now I know that I read somewhere that. . . ." If you have a bit of discipline and can use a database program, you can save lots of frustration because you can't remember where you read it.

I have one colleague who actually was disciplined enough to do this and has used her bibliography effectively. Since grad school, she has put together a bibliography of more than five thousand items, and she did a good job of keeping track of all the publication information. She uses it regularly when she writes for filling in her citations. She did make one mistake, however. What she acknowledges that she did wrong was not to make it an *annotated* bibliography. An annotated bibliography includes any notes you might have taken on the work. It can be a series of phrases, full sentences, or even abstracts. My colleague admits that as she reads more, she tends to forget more. She may recall that she read a particular work, but not necessarily what it was about in any detail. She wishes she had included annotations.

If you regularly take notes on what you read, you are already more than halfway there on compiling an annotated bibliography.

Certainly, you can keep your notes in file folders or notebooks, but a better bet is to enter the information on some form of database program. Doing so will help immensely when you write, especially as you build your career. The sooner you start, the better, but it's never too late!

BIBLIOGRAPHIC SOFTWARE

If you are adept at building relational databases, you could design your own bibliographic database. These are powerful, and you can include lots of information about each source. But why go to the trouble?

Almost since the beginning of word processing on desktops, a number of bibliographic software programs have been available for relatively little money. Many are good and constantly improving. Each scholar probably has unique needs, but some general features ought to be considered. Several offer bibliographic styles for archaeology and anthropology, including those associated with the journals *American Antiquity* and *American Anthropologist*. The most useful have a user interface linked directly to your word processor as well as web connectivity and searching. For what features should you look?

Start with the size of database the product will hold. Certainly, for a personal bibliography, many products mentioned will easily handle most needs, holding many thousand references. On the other hand, it might be useful to build a lab or office annotated bibliography, which might require a product that will handle substantially more references. Look for a product that can handle a relatively large comment field or text field in addition to the basic reference information. This will allow you to put in all your notes on each source. If you are limited in the number of characters of text you can enter, avoid the product!

You probably already know this, but *data fields* are the pieces of information you enter, such as publisher location, author last name, or publication date. Find a product that will allow you to alter the names of data fields, delete certain fields, or add new ones. Look for a product that has lots of bibliographic styles, particularly for archaeology or anthropology. These templates are already formatted in the style of the journal and allow you quickly to set up bibliographies/references cited sections of your paper just by entering the author name/date in your text. Find a product that will allow you to import files from another bibliographic product easily. If you decide to change programs, you won't have to do lots of work to change products.

STYLES GUIDES AND WHERE TO FIND THEM

Few technical matters cause professors and students, or contractors and contract managers, more grief than reference and citation styles, but there are other concerns for style as well, such as how illustrations get treated, measurement systems, and use of numbers. Stylistic differences may seem minimal, often just punctuation or capitalization. However, if you pay attention to these elements up front, you'll be the darling of copyeditors and save a lot of time.

The single-best approach is to model your manuscript according to what the journal, publisher, agency, or professor wants. Usually journals will have a style guide, sometimes published in the back of every issue, sometimes published as a somewhat lengthy document periodically, and, more frequently these days, on websites for the journal. For American archaeology, the de facto standard is *American Antiquity* (used for this volume and series), published in *American Antiquity* (1992, 57:749–70) and on the Web at www.saa.org/Publications/StyleGuide/ styframe.html. However, other journals do use other approaches, so you are well advised to look for the style guide for the journal before submitting a manuscript.

Certain book publishers prefer certain styles. Many, for example, will tell authors to use the *Chicago Manual of Style* for a guide or to follow MLA (Modern Language Association) or APA (American Psychological Association), of which most anthropological styles are variations. Certain agencies, such as the United States Department of Defense, may also have preferred styles for reports done under contract with them.

The simple rule of thumb before you write is to find out whether there is a preferred style and follow it. This will save you lots of time and grief later. If you cannot find a style guide, or if it doesn't cover the kind of source you have cited, look at a recent issue of the publication to see whether you can find how similar sources have been treated (this has been a problem for Internet and other electronic sources), and follow that approach. In fact, if you can't figure out *any* source from the style guide, do the same thing. You'll usually come out fine.

CONCLUSION

So many of the research and writing tools discussed in this chapter have changed because of computers, especially with word processing, and these days only the rare archaeologist doesn't use them. Still, some remain intimidated by the technology. In chapter 5, we'll consider core issues about archaeological computing and presenting the past.

5

 COMPUTERS AND PRESENTING
THE PAST

Tips on writing fill books. As tough as writing can be, for some archaeologists the physical act of putting words to paper is more daunting. Many have to do their first drafts with pen and paper, handwriting giving them time to think and create. Others prefer writing's buggy whip, the typewriter. Some prefer dictation, usually to their secretary's chagrin. Most of us use computers and word processors these days, not to mention lots of other associated software and hardware. There is no good reason here to cover much about computers; plenty of sources are available, from good computer magazines loaded with tips to online sources that cover just about everything you could want to know about computers. More important, rapid technological change dates all these subjects very quickly.

Few sources are directed specifically at archaeological computing, but a good recent one is McPherron and Dibble's (2002) *Using Computers in Archaeology: A Practical Guide.* Much of the book is about computers in field archaeology, from total stations to GPS, but one chapter considers digital publication, looking at such topics as platforms and file formats and issues surrounding them. For specific computer applications, the *Dummies* and *Idiot's Guide* series are actually pretty good starting places, but you won't find many references to archaeology in them. Some of the best computer-related material specific to archaeology has appeared in the Society for American Archaeology's *Bulletin,* now the *SAA Archaeological Record.*

Some archaeologists seem to have strange attitudes about computers, but computers are neither sorcerer's apprentice nor savior. Computers are really nothing all that special, but from the way many of us talk, you would believe they are magic. Most of us seem to have a love–hate relationship with technology that has caused us to lust after the latest and best computers at the same time that many of us are afraid of them.

We'd be far better off if we could get past the awe of computers. To help, let's try to pin down some key ideas about using them. These aren't hard and fast, but they may help you when it comes to figuring out what you need to use computers effectively in your writing or in other tasks of presenting the past.

BASIC COMPUTER SKILLS YOU'LL NEED

Although these may seem a bit silly as basic skills, the number of people who have problems with them is surprising. To use computers well, you will need to pick up these skills:

- Learn to type reasonably well.
- Become adept at using the mouse, touch pad, trackball, or other method for moving the cursor around the screen.
- Learn to RTFM (geek for "read the f*#$ing manual).
- Learn something about file structure, directories, and pathways used by your computer.

These skills will take you a long way toward mastering computers and the software you will need to accomplish what you wish.

ADVANCED SKILLS YOU'LL NEED

People who are mystified by computers think that every new piece of equipment or software is something unique that has to be learned with a great expenditure of energy and four-letter words. The truth is that much of what you need to learn is similar to what you have already learned. Macs are similar in operation to PCs running on Windows; Word is similar to other word processors; Photoshop is similar to many other image programs. So if you want to be skilled at computer use, you'll need to do the following:

- Find out what is similar in a computer or application to what you already have used, and what is different.

- Learn how to follow digital or hard-copy tutorial materials available from the manufacturer or through third parties.
- Learn enough to call technical support or a geek friend if you hit a real snag.

When it actually comes to learning new programs, many think that a class will help them. A class may give basics, but what learning software or hardware takes is mostly just sitting down and "playing" until you reach a comfort level or until you can make it do what you want.

COMPUTER HARDWARE

The odds are good that you will work in a situation where you will use computer hardware that is already on your desk. If you are buying your own computer or are afforded the opportunity to get new equipment, you may find yourself in a quandary about what to get. Should that be the case, think about the following issues:

- *What will your primary uses for the computer be?* In archaeology we still have to word-process, use e-mail, develop databases, and budget on spreadsheets. You will want a computer that handles these tasks with reasonable speed, which is just about any newer computer. If you want to do anything with graphics, you'll want a faster computer with a larger monitor, a big hard drive, and probably a rewritable CD or DVD drive.
- *Will your primary usage be in the office, home, or field?* If you travel much or are in the field a great deal, you might consider buying a laptop instead of a desktop. Archaeological fieldwork is not the best place for any computer unless it is specifically protected against harsh conditions, especially dust and rain. Having both is the best of both worlds, but if you decide on a laptop and use it in the field, protect it!
- *What kinds of computers are used in your office and at home?* You'll find that compatibility is useful, so you may want to be sure that platforms/operating systems are the same in both places.
- *What is your budget for buying hardware?* Buy the fastest processor, biggest hard drive, and largest monitor you can afford. Remember that the most expensive equipment is the fastest and biggest, so if one or two steps down in technology will do, you

probably won't notice the difference and will save money. Also remember that the equipment will be cheaper and out-of-date tomorrow.

- *What peripherals might be useful?* We archaeologists like our toys, and computers are great playgrounds. Depending on needs and budget, you can put just about everything you want into and onto your computer. Computer toys can also be outrageous money and time sinks, but some peripherals such as printers are necessities. If you will work with images, you may need large-capacity, rewritable storage devices such as CD and/or DVD drives, scanners, and a range of other hardware. When you consider these devices, also factor in costs of media, printer cartridges, and other expendable supplies. Much depends on what you are going to do, and specific software may require specific hardware to operate and to output results.

TACTICS FOR BUYING HARDWARE

If you've answered these questions and have a good notion of what you need and what you want, then it's time for some detective work. Frankly, word of mouth is not such a bad way to find out about the quality of products, service, and support. Ask around. If the product is specifically for archaeology, ask other archaeologists who might know the product. If information technologists are on staff, ask them what they like to work with (and fix!).

Read reviews. You can find these in numerous computer magazines and online. Many of them will also give you a good idea of what you might find for "street price" as opposed to retail.

Finally, a bit of advice: Once you've bought, stop looking! You'll always find a cheaper price tomorrow.

SOFTWARE

The latest hardware means nothing unless you have the software to make it do what you want. In some ways, software is much more difficult to discuss because of the vast variety, much greater than the hardware. Some of the same questions about hardware apply to software, especially those related to your uses and compatibility within an office or home.

TRY BEFORE YOU BUY

Although software is generally cheaper than hardware, most of it is still expensive, especially when it comes to specialty software such as statistics, mapping, graphics, or Geographic Information Systems (GIS). You owe it to yourself and/or your organization to investigate before you buy. Control the urge to buy software on a whim just because it looks cool. Explore these alternatives:

- Borrow a copy from a friend, but only to try. If you like it, buy a legal copy.
- Try shareware. You can often download a program, see whether it works for you, and then register the copy by paying a fee.
- Try "lite" and demo versions of the software that you download and try out for a period of time, often thirty days, or a number of uses before you have to buy a copy. Go to the company website to see whether it offers demo copies for download and trial.
- Try freeware, programs produced and distributed for free, but sometimes paid for by advertisements that appear on your screen. You can sometimes get rid of ads if you pay a fee for the "pro" version. Some freeware also may not be full-featured.
- If you are on a college or university campus, the local bookstore or campus computer center may offer academic pricing or may have purchased a site license that can save many dollars.
- Read reviews of software before you buy anything.

LEARNING CURVES

A *learning curve* is the amount of time and energy required to learn a piece of hardware or software. If you are not at all familiar with a type of software, learning curves can be extremely steep. Once you've learned the basics, the curve flattens a bit, so learning becomes easier. If you buy new hardware or software, plan on spending time learning it. There really are no shortcuts. Classes, tutorials, *Dummies* and *Idiots* books, or software can be helpful, but in the end you just have to go through the product systematically. Remember, however, that most of your skills and knowledge from one piece of hardware or software are often transferable to another.

Ultimately if you need help, don't be afraid to ask for it, but your local computer guru will be more inclined to help if you've really tried first. You might consider three *T*'s with software: *try, toy,* and *trouble.* When you get new software, install it and just *try* it. Look for similar constructions to like products you know. See what's different. Then *toy* with it—just play with it! This gives you some familiarity with moving around in the system. Take a document or image created with a prior version or a similar product, and see how compatible the old version is with the new or how the new product handles it. Then *trouble* your way through the product. Use it on something you need to create or do. You may need to use the help screens or worry your way through the tutorial or manual. Sometimes even third-party manuals can help. *Try* and *toy* are fun; *trouble* isn't. When you've done this, you'll probably have figured things out. Then, practice what you've learned regularly and often—use it or lose it!

CONCLUSION

More than anything else in presenting the past, computers have changed the ways in which we deal with images, the subject of the next chapter. Computers show up again in a discussion of digital imaging. You just can't escape them!

6

VISUAL ARCHAEOLOGY

Visual archaeology is any use of illustrative materials in support of archaeological presentation. Given that archaeological writing is about as dry as the dirt we usually dig, most of us won't quibble about the importance of images to our work. We rely heavily on slides for our conference or public talks, we zing our colleagues about the quality of artifact illustrations in their site reports, and we fiddle with new ways to provide better images to present our work. By and large, we do visual archaeology badly. Unless you've been very fortunate in your training, the odds are slim that you've had a course or even part of one on creating and using illustrations or other graphics with your work. Even more of a problem is that most of us don't really give much thought to our visuals until we are getting ready for our final report, a conference paper, or a Rotary luncheon talk.

As with writing and public speaking, the visual part of archaeology was something else you were apparently supposed to learn by osmosis. Some field methods volumes have chapters on field photography (see Heizer and Graham 1967:148–57 or Hester, Shafer, and Feder 1997:159–76 for good examples), but the coverage is minimal. Mostly it is geared toward field recording, where the emphasis is on data ordination, not presentation. Other works on both photography and drawing have been specific to artifact classes or techniques. Most of us have had to pick up skills by taking outside classes or just by doing them. As with many other skills used in archaeology, we should recognize that being an illustrator or photographer could be a full-time occupation. Sadly, we also know that most project budgets can't afford a site photographer, and most labs can't put a full-time artist on staff. As with many other parts of our jobs, we end up doing most of the work by our poorly trained selves.

If that's where you find yourself, you should at least know some basics and some sources. The intent here is in no way to cover all there is to know about visual archaeology. Rather, we'll look into some core theoretical and practical aspects of the use of images and provide some basic tools to get you started. The chapter will touch on photography, drawing, computer graphics, and video, but not in much detail, and mostly to provide source materials. Each topic could be a book and probably several!

THE CULTURAL LIFE OF IMAGES

Images are vastly more complex than most of us think. As Molyneaux (1997:1) notes, "Understanding a picture requires the education and direction of attention to its meaningful aspects." As he goes on to consider, images in scientific illustration by way of appearing to be exactly what they represent—the way we think we use illustration and photography in archaeology—claim truth to nature and science but are nonetheless saturated with meaning (Molyneaux 1997:3). The pictures and drawings we create and select are not value-neutral; they reflect our theoretical approaches, our aesthetic sense, and even our budgets. We should pay more attention to just what it is that images say about us as archaeologists, our profession, and our concern for our audiences, not just what we think they say about the archaeological record.

To do this is not all that easy, but we at least need to think about how we create and use images. At very least we should keep the following points in mind:

- Each image should be chosen to support or amplify a point made by the text of a report or your presentation.
- Images should not be "filler."
- As with the text, images need to be chosen with the audience in mind.
- Consider the values connoted by each image.

Illustrations of both sites and artifacts have a history at least as ancient as their first appearance in medieval manuscripts, but generally the development of archaeological illustration parallels the development of archaeology, and both are tied to the development of technology to produce the illustrations. Piggott's (1979) *Antiquity Depicted: Aspects of Archaeological Illustration* provides a good history, but the general trend has been from topographical recording, to drawing of excavations, to drawings and engravings of artifacts, to photography of both, to digital recording and manipulation. Photography also has an early beginning, traceable back to the photographs of W. H. Fox Talbot of manuscripts, engravings, and busts in England. By the 1850s, photography was regarded as a panacea for problems of documenting materials, but it was followed by disillusion when scholars realized that photos could distort evidence (Dorrell 1989:1). Whatever the problems with photography, it certainly became part of the standard techniques for recording artifacts and features in the field and laboratory by the late 1800s.

Illustration of representative artifacts has always been an important element in good communication about the past. Certainly photographic documentation is useful and necessary, but for detail about the skill of the flint knapper or pot maker, nothing is as good as excellent illustration. Some might say that photos are more "authentic" or real, but all graphics are in some way representation of three dimensions in two. In both drawings and photographs, for example, certain elements can be (de)emphasized by the angle of light, shadowing, and distance from the object. As Piggott (1978:7) notes, "The form of illustration cannot be divorced from its purpose and the requirements of the society in which the given visual language gains currency."

In discussing Piggott's statement, Adkins and Adkins (1989:1) say that illustration needs to be tailored to the audience and to the purpose of the illustration before a "level of technology" used to execute the illustration can be decided. Upon deciding on these elements, the illustrator has little room for "maneuver" except in how the variables change. Reading the Adkinses' history of archaeological illustration is instructive, especially in their discussion of the impact of photography. They clearly demonstrate that "archaeological illustrations are interpretive diagrams rather than attempts at realistic or artistic portrayal" (Adkins and Adkins 1989:7–8).

PHOTOGRAPHS VERSUS DRAWINGS

Photographs are deceptive. They seem to be realistic in that they record all that is visible to the lens of the camera and capable of being recorded on film or digital media. They can be manipulated, especially if they are digital, but they are essentially not very selective. They do not convey all of reality and, in fact, miss lots of important information and include irrelevant information. Their weakness is that they present all information "equally."

Drawings, on the other hand are selective from the start, emphasizing details the illustrator and archaeologist want the reader to see. They are interpretive, meant to convey key information about an artifact or feature. Drawings can also be an aid to study (Dillon 1985:6) because they force close observation, with constant reference to the object and lots of handling, rechecking, and measurements.

As it does with text, the intended audience dictates the kind of drawings used. Some of the conventions used in archaeological drawings, like technical jargon, may not be meaningful to nonspecialists. Use of drawings or photographs may also be a function of cost. Generally the cost of producing both has gone down. In terms of production, drawings are probably more expensive in terms of production time, but they can convey substantially greater amounts of information. Photographs are relatively easy to take, especially if they are digital, and manipulation of images has gotten easier. Layout and printing costs of photographs used to be prohibitive, which is why some archaeologists used line drawings for artifacts, but current technologies, particularly using desktop publishing tools, allow relatively inexpensive layout and printing of both. Color drawings and photographs are still costly to print.

Archaeologists have a substantially greater number of ways to present information by using illustrations than they did a few decades ago. Choice of graphic media should be made on the basis of both intended audience and the sort of information to be conveyed to the audience, not ease of production or cost. Consider these issues carefully as you decide.

TOOLS

Having the right tools is important to just about everything we do in archaeology, and that's no different with visual archaeology. One can get by with few and inexpensive tools, but quality does show in illustrations. Good tools do not make good illustrations, but they help!

SOURCES FOR ARCHAEOLOGICAL DRAWING

Several books provide a good coverage of archaeological drawing. Adkins and Adkins' (1989) *Archaeological Illustration* is perhaps the most thorough. Their volume discusses a bit of history and theory of archaeological illustration, as well as considering equipment, drawing under a range of conditions including the field and lab, and drawing different kinds of artifacts and features. Their next to last chapter is especially relevant to this volume with coverage of drawing for a wide range of reproduction types, from print to other media such as slides, microfiche, and overheads. They also look at matters of copyright, but more current material about it is online.

Still useful is *The Student's Guide to Archaeological Illustrating* (Dillon 1985) in the UCLA Institute of Archaeology's Archaeological Research Tools series. The articles focus on particular types of illustrations or artifacts. Especially useful is Armstrong's (1985) chapter on drawing maps.

The most complete coverage of drawing any artifact type is Addington's (1986) *Lithic Illustration: Drawing Flaked Stone Artifacts for Publication*. Her last chapter on the working relationship of the archaeologist and the illustrator should perhaps be read first. Its two pages provide a quick study on how to work with a specialist.

A little book by Brodribb (1971) called *Drawing Archaeological Finds* may be the best small book on illustration. The book is organized around the process of drawing, and that helps one to understand its complexities. In fact, more than anything else from all these books, the most useful element novices may get from them is to understand the *process* of drawing.

Support is also available from a professional organization of archaeological illustrators, the Association of Archaeological Illustrators and Surveyors, an international body for those engaged in all aspects of professional archaeological illustration and survey. They produce a journal, *Graphic Archaeology*, newsletter, and website (www.aais.org.uk/). They have also developed a series of technical papers for drawing lithics, pottery, wooden artifacts, and a number of different artifacts classes.

EQUIPMENT FOR DRAWING

All the books list equipment that you might need for drawing. As might be expected, different tools may be needed for different types of drawings, and there are a lot of tools. Adkins and Adkins (1989:11–39) not only list the equipment but also detail uses and varieties. Much of the equipment is relatively inexpensive, but special drawing tools can be expensive. If you intend to produce in-house drawings, you can build your collection of equipment over time. Certainly some of the equipment listed has been overtaken by technological change.

SOURCES FOR ARCHAEOLOGICAL PHOTOGRAPHY

Very basic information on photography in the field is available in chapters in the widely used field methods guides (Heizer and Graham 1967:148–57; Hester, Shafer, and Feder 1997:159–76). Of use in them is description of different kinds of field photos (site views, features, underwater, etc.) and the use of visible scales in photos, as well as some issues with special types of photos, such as with petroglyphs.

More detailed coverage is available in Dorrell's (1989) *Photography in Archaeology and Conservation.* He includes a good history and then looks at specific issues of photography in the field and lab, with a chapter on preparing materials for publication. Though dated, this chapter raises important issues regarding the use of 35mm transparencies in publication, especially color balance between slides. What is apparent is that anyone should seek the advice of a potential publisher regarding the type and quality of photos to be used.

A Practical Guide to Archaeological Photography by Howell and Blanc (1992) may be the best place to start if you haven't done much photography. After a fair coverage of camera function and ways to use light, the guide looks at photography in both the field and laboratory. The last chapter, "Review," is something you should look at even if you are experienced. It has "index cards" that are worth the trouble to copy if you can't afford a copy of the book itself. The seventeen cards contain topically organized, bulleted lists of key elements about everything from how to shoot artifacts to f-stops and depth of field. Appendix D contains a somewhat useful series of points about preparing slide presentations.

In truth, if you are a novice to photography, starting with the guides listed here might not be as effective as very basic guides on photography such as *Photography for Dummies* (Hart and Richards 1998). If you are more skilled, you might like to see what professional photographers say about archaeological site and artifact photography. An article in *American Archaeology* (Anonymous 2001) features limited advice from Eldon Leiter, Jerry Jacka, David Whitley, and Steven Wall. The advice is interesting, and the article makes the point that photography is an art that takes years of experience to do well.

DIGITAL PHOTOGRAPHY

Rapid improvements in digital imaging have dramatically increased the quality and utility of digital photography in both the field and lab. Combined with digital scanning and a range of software to manipulate the images you generate, there is not much you can't do with images, and the gap between drawing and photography can be readily bridged.

Little in basic source materials for archaeology discusses digital photography. Although the seventh edition of *Field Methods in Archaeology* (Hester, Shafer, and Feder 1997:166) mentions digital photography, the material is minimal and dated. A more current overview appears in McPherron and Dibble's (2002:160–77) *Using Computers in Archaeology: A Practical Guide.* Most useful discussion of what can be done is in the fringe literature of notes and newsletters. An article by Rick (1999) provides a recent survey of digital cameras in archaeology, with good coverage of the technology and several key issues in their use. It's now true that for almost every purpose in archaeological presentation except slides and enlargements above 11 × 14 inches, digital photography equals or surpasses film photography.

DIGITAL IMAGING

Digital cameras derive their strength from the connection to the computer and its use in manipulating images. On a superficial level, computer graphics—that is, digital imaging—is really easy. You can quickly learn to scan or use a digital camera or grab an image off the web, but doing more with them requires substantially greater knowledge. The learning curve is as steep as any in computing, short of learning to program. Graphics may be tougher in that using them effectively also requires a level of artistic skill most of us either don't have or haven't developed. There is no way to cover the topic thoroughly here, so we'll just touch on the basics, looking at what you might need for digital imaging. A digital camera, a scanner, and a graphics program are the core of a digital imaging system.

DIGITAL CAMERAS

A digital camera, as the name implies, stores images digitally rather than using film. Once you take a picture, you can download it to a computer and manipulate it with your graphics program. Digital cameras are now relatively commonplace, with quality improving and prices dropping. The resolution of digital cameras is limited by camera memory, the optical resolution of the mechanism that digitizes the image, and the output device used to show the picture.

At present, the best digital cameras are not capable of producing film-quality resolution, although this is changing dramatically. The greatest advantage of digital cameras is that you avoid the film process altogether. For fieldwork, this has huge advantages because you can see almost instantly whether you've got the picture you want and retake if you need to. Because there is no film or processing cost, you can take lots of pictures at extremely low cost, amortizing the higher cost of the camera and media very quickly. For presentation, you can get reasonably high-quality images and easily download, manipulate, and incorporate them into websites, CD-ROMs, and publications.

SCANNERS

A scanner is a must for anyone, and prices are so low that some package computer deals even come with a scanner. Scanners are the computer equivalent of a copy machine, but the items being copied are digitized so that your computer can read them. Scanners provide a convenient way for entering text and graphics on your computer. Even most low-end scanners have software that will allow you to scan and manipulate graphics, as well as optical character recognition (OCR) software that will convert scanned text into text your word processor will read.

Scanners come in a range of forms. Pen and other hand-held scanners can read a line or more of text at a time as you move over it. Their benefit is portability, but their drawback is speed. Some scanners require that a sheet of paper be pulled though the mechanism. They offer portability, but if you need to scan from a book, they are impractical. Flatbed scanners are the best bet for most purposes. They come in a range of sizes and have a flat glass surface on which you lay a document or picture. A moving light source, much like that in a copy machine, captures the image.

Digital cameras and scanners have other important uses. They can actually be used to help create "drawings" of three-dimensional objects. One can scan or photograph artifacts such as pottery sherds or stone tools and then use a graphics program to eliminate or enhance certain elements of the object, much as one might do with a drawing. Houk and Moses (1998) discuss the process using a scanner, but it is similar with a digital camera.

OTHER TOOLS

You might also find the following pieces of equipment useful:

- *Slide or negative scanner.* Most scanners do not allow 35mm color transparencies (slides) or negatives to be scanned well. Specialized scanners do a better job.
- *Web camera.* Attached directly to your computer, web cams allow you to photograph and input images from the real world to the World Wide Web.
- *Graphics tablets.* You can draw with a pencillike stylus on a touch-sensitive pad and have what you create put into your computer for modification in a graphics program, bypassing paper drawings altogether.
- *Graphics programs.* These allow you to take the images generated by a scanner or camera and manipulate them with your computer. Simplified programs for graphics and OCR (which allows you to scan text) usually come bundled with the scanner or camera. These are usually a limited or "light" edition (LE), meaning that the program is not full featured or may not be as capable of handling the data. Most bundled graphics software allows you to resize, rotate, crop, and do minor adjustments to the images. Some even allow you to compress the file size of image files for e-mailing and web use. However, if you want to do more with images or work with large images, even isolate elements of images, a higher-end graphics program is best. Most such programs will probably do more than you can use, but in addition to the features of the LE software, you will want to have some level of color and brightness/contrast adjustment, the ability to put text and draw directly onto the image, and the ability to reduce the size of the image file for easy use on the World Wide Web or for e-mail. Without trying to explain it in detail here, you may also wish to be able to move back and forth between the two main systems of dealing with images, vector and

raster graphics, particularly if you do work in GIS. Finally, you'll want a program that allows you to prepare both print and electronic images, so find one that allows you to use and convert between a range of image formats. There is a wide range of image formats, with three standards in common use on the web, but many in use for print media. For print, the formats are more variable, and certain publishers prefer certain formats. Most high-end programs handle all the common formats.

SPECIALTY GRAPHICS PROGRAMS

Beyond these graphics basics, even discussing graphics gets complicated, especially with issues such as raster versus vector images, file formats, and file compression (see McPherron and Dibble 2002:160–70 for a brief discussion). Some issues are program-specific.

Preparing images for the web brings even more presentation choices. One element that many people like to put on web pages is animation or movement. You can make simple animated images with free and shareware programs, and some graphics programs also include animation. High-end specialty programs allow for creation of extremely sophisticated animations without dramatically increasing file size, though some require special plug-ins or players (downloadable for free) to see the animation.

Other programs allow you to sketch an object, and then have it turned into a real image. Computer-aided design and drafting (CADD) programs may become very useful if you are working with architects and engineers on a CRM project, but good ones are very expensive, with steep learning curves. If you need CADD, perhaps some other part of your organization has a useful program. GIS programs also contain specialty applications that allow you to produce images to better comprehend the patterning present in data. In the realm of the web, some programs allow you to build three-dimensional images (actually, they are quasi-3D; see Rick and Hart 1997 for a discussion of processes and possibilities). Some programs are set up specifically to allow you to build buttons and navigation tools for the web.

If computer graphics interest you, just go to a computer store and look around, go online, or look at any of several magazines having to do with graphics. Most specialty graphics programs are relatively expensive, so get reviews, talk to other users, and use trial software downloadable from the web before you buy.

VIDEO

Videos and films are just about the closest approximation to real life. They are also a very good way to educate at the same time that we entertain, and they are media our publics generally prefer over others. At the same time, they are probably the media archaeologists have the least experience producing. They have been relatively expensive, film especially so. Many archaeologists have used video in the field to document activities and sites, but they have rarely taken more than "home movies" because of the expense and skill required. However, changes in technology, especially digital camcorders and relatively easy-to-use editing software, now allow archaeologists to produce video near professional quality.

Because video seems to be a recording of real life, audiences might think that what they see is closer to reality or somehow more authentic than other kinds of presentation. The truth is, however, that video is subject to the same biases as other images, a limitation we should remember and of which we should inform our audiences. Although little has been written about archaeological video and film, there is a solid body of literature about ethnographic film from which to draw. Heider's (1976; 2001:426–33) work provides a good starting point regarding theoretical issues, many of them applying to archaeological film.

STORYBOARDING

Among the more difficult issues is the fact that text is linear, but pictures are not. In video, nonlinear pictures must be crunched into what is essentially a linear text, a script. Storyboarding can help the process. In storyboarding, the point of view of the camera and the action are linked by putting them onto storyboards, or drawings of how the story should be told. The storyboarding process is also very useful in developing multimedia product, a subject that will be discussed in chapter 12.

GETTING YOUR PRODUCTION NOTICED

Even if you do video on a shoestring budget, distributing the product is not cheap. Sponsored by Archaeological Legacy Institute, the Archaeology Channel (TAC) at www.archaeologychannel.org partners with producers of archaeological video or film and broadcasts the films using streaming media on the web (it does the same for audio materials). If nothing else, TAC is a good place to find out what is going on in archaeology video, and it can be a relatively inexpensive way to distribute your productions.

Although archaeologists have tried artifact drawings and most have done photographs, making a quality video without help is probably well outside our abilities. Because we recognize video as a useful medium for communicating with the public, we will usually have such work done by professionals. When it comes to presenting the past, perhaps it is time to consider what we do to be as much a product of teamwork with specialists and consultants as it is in our field- and lab work, the subject of chapter 7.

7

LONE RANGER OR TEAM PLAYER?

If all the tasks archaeologists are called upon to do haven't scared you by now, you must be a better person than most! The problem for archaeologists is that our field is so vast that we tend to become jacks-of-all-trades and masters of none. A few of us may have had time to develop a specialization, but we have to know something about almost every aspect of our discipline, from how to do surveying to how to analyze faunal remains collected from a site. Many of us can know something about many of these things, but often just enough to be dangerous! The same is true when it comes to presenting the past. Many of the tasks, such as basic write-up, are relatively straightforward, but do we really have the time and intellectual capacity to learn photography, graphics, CD-ROM development, and broadband web technologies? True, one can know about all these things and maybe even do a few of them reasonably well, but the end product usually will not be as good as you might like.

We have gotten to the point in our field- and lab work that we are comfortable with hiring specialists as consultants, even to the point of building them into our bids for projects and our grant budgets. At the same time, most of us rarely consider the similar situation when we come to preparing the final report on our project, even for the illustrations. We try to do it alone, and because of that, our product is often less than it could be, and sometimes less than it should be. If you are fortunate enough to work in a large operation, your overhead costs may include hiring illustrators, photographers, and web designers, but if you are like many, you just can't afford these specialists and still be competitive in the CRM world. If you want to improve the product and can consider a team approach to presenting the past, what kinds of people should you get, and how do you find them?

DEVELOPING THE TEAM

As you hire staff for projects, you almost always consider a range of qualifications. You need to hire people who are good in the field at a variety of tasks, from personnel management to excavation. You also want to know that they can handle themselves in the lab. As already noted, you probably will want people who are capable of writing the reports on the projects to which they are assigned. At the same time, you might consider putting a qualification in a job ad for someone who can also illustrate or do web design or some other task related to presenting the past. If you get lucky, you might be able to assemble a pretty good team.

If you work in a university, you may have a plethora of low-cost but fairly skilled student labor at your disposal, people who need to build their résumés or portfolios for future employment. Most universities also have people who "hang around" long after getting their degrees, just because they like the university atmosphere. They survive by working at temporary assignments or low-paying hourly jobs, but they are nonetheless highly skilled.

If you plan on building a CRM or academic laboratory, you should do some longer-term planning and work toward hiring a specialized staff. Some of us have built report preparation into budgets for many years; even a small survey project has a line item for the task. Target all or some portion of the report preparation money from all the projects toward hiring an illustrator, computer specialist, or whatever you most need at the time. Also consider building in some of each contract's overhead or indirect costs to include hiring these people. If you happen to be in a situation where you can request permanent employees as budget lines, then build toward adding staff according to your presentation needs, just as you would for field- or laboratory work.

Figuring out what kinds of people you will need can be difficult, and much depends on your office or program's goals. You should spend some time planning how to develop such a team. What do you most need? Consider adding the following team members:

- *Editor/copyeditor.* As much as most of us might like to think we are great writers, everyone can be improved by editing. Good editors have many skills, but they pay more attention to detail than most people. They must know spelling and grammar but also need to be able to work within archaeological styles and standards. They should also be good at proofreading. With enough experience in archaeology, they might even be able to do indexing well.
- *Illustrator/graphics specialist.* People with an ability to draw, and in ways that you want them to, are important to any team. The trick is in finding someone willing to learn what is important to show in his or her illustrations, based on collaboration with an archaeologist. These team members need to understand that what they are doing is not "art" in the sense that they must follow reasonable standards of archaeological illustration. These days, they should also have some level of experience with computer graphics, not just drawing.
- *Designer.* You may be fortunate enough to find an illustrator who also has skill at design. Design is what some might call the layout of a report, posters, your website, or any graphics product that comes from your office. Designers help set a style for the products and your whole office. They also must have facility with computer graphics.
- *Digital media specialist.* If you need to develop an office or company website, or if you wish to present materials electronically, you may wish to hire an individual capable of working with digital media. Such a person does not necessarily need a degree in computer science. Most computer science programs don't teach the kinds of skills needed to do work with the web or CD-ROMs. As important are people skills; digital media specialists must listen to be able to carry out the media goals of those in your office. They can't be the stereotypical computer geek and do well at the job. Skills with specific computer programs for the web or graphics are crucial, but they don't need to be able to field-strip a computer!
- *Photographer.* Many archaeologists consider photography to be just an extension of note taking. We are often not very good at taking pictures, which shows at lots of conference presentations. Basic skills are not too hard to learn, but much beyond that takes training and experience. High-budget projects may be able to hire photographers for the field, but most forget about it for the lab. Consider what bad photos might tell a client about your operation. These days, a photographer should be adept at both film and digital

photography to be useful to your organization. You might also want this team member to know about, or learn, video.

- *Instructional designer/educational specialist.* Many of us have spent more time than we like to remember in academic settings. We've taken lots of formal courses and may even have taken additional training in workshops. We've developed a feeling for when instruction is good or bad. That doesn't mean, however, that we have the skill to design and execute a good course. We may need help. Many archaeology organizations do some level of instruction, from teaching skills to staff members to working on certification programs for avocational archaeologists. For instruction delivered at a distance electronically or through correspondence, design becomes even more crucial. Individuals who develop such materials must have training or substantial experience in constructing, packaging, and delivering educational products. As important, they have to learn what it is they are producing, so they must have some level of experience with archaeology.
- *Public relations/marketing specialist.* How do you let your publics know what you are producing or what events you are planning unless you have someone doing advertising for your products? This topic is covered in detail in chapter 11.

OUTSOURCING WORK OR HIRING IN-HOUSE

You can probably think of some other specialists to add to the list of people you could use in your office. If you just consider the positions listed here, you'll quickly realize that the annual costs would be well in excess of $300,000, a figure most CRM firms or university labs just can't afford when most can't even pay for core archaeological specialists like geomorphologists! This means that you either must have your archaeology staff develop the skills as a sideline to their regular chores or must outsource the work or hire temporary staff to do the tasks in-house. You will probably have to outsource for specific tasks on projects, anyway, so why not do so with much of your presentation work?

If you are in this situation, consider the costs and benefits. Costs for hiring short-term consultants or specialists are generally higher per hour than having specialists on your staff. At the same time, paying salaried staff also includes benefit costs, and you pay for any downtime when you don't have work for them. As you may already know from your fieldwork when you hire consultants, these folks are outsiders. They know that they are contributing to a product, but they may not feel they are part of the team and may not fully understand your approaches and goals.

If you outsource work, you need to pay particular attention to making these consultants understand your project's goals. While the scientific specialists we bring in have often set themselves up to work specifically with archaeologists, most of the consultants you bring in to help with presentation probably have a wide range of clients for whom they work. Good consultants also realize this problem and work hard to understand your needs and goals, sometimes to the point of being annoying (this is actually a good trait in a consultant). If they don't ask lots of questions, they probably aren't going to be a good consultant. Achieving good relationships and understanding does take your time and work, but if consultants work for you regularly, they eventually develop a feel for your needs.

Finding such people can often be difficult. If your are part of a university, consider yourself lucky in that most universities have a wide range of offices specifically designed to provide consulting services in every presentation specialty listed earlier. In some cases, you buy their services at an hourly rate, and they can even produce the final products you need, such as 1,500 copies of a CD-ROM or 30 copies of a contract report. If you work in the private sector but near a university, you can often use university services, probably at rates competitive with, or even a bit lower than, private business. If you need to hire services from the private sector, you can try a number of approaches to finding quality consultants. You can ask colleagues or competitors whom they use. Competitors may be hesitant to tell you, but that's not very likely. You can ask each potential service provider for references and samples of his or her work. You can ask for competitive bids from several providers, and probably should. You may even enjoy being on the other side of the bid process for a change!

Whatever the case, you will need to be clear about your needs, and you need to make your consultants part of a team if you can. If you find good consultants who figure out your needs and how best to work within your style and structure, you'll obviously want to go back to them. The better the situation for them in terms of working conditions and clarity of goals, the better work you'll get. If you go back to them often, you may find that all your costs go down, in both time and money, especially if you treat them with respect. This should go without saying, but consultants have skills you need, and they are professionals who deserve as much respect for their skills and knowledge as anyone else associated with your project.

8

PUBLISH OR PERISH? COMMUNICATING WITH COLLEAGUES

Communicating your work to colleagues is a crucial element of your work as an archaeologist. Doing good archaeology demands a dependence on other archaeologists who provide feedback about your work. However, colleagues may also be your most critical audience, some of them even your direct competitors, competing for contracts, positions, and reputations. For those in academic positions, communicating with professional colleagues is a key to earning promotion and tenure. For CRM archaeologists, if you don't produce reports, you don't eat!

Certainly, one can communicate with colleagues, as we often do, over a beer at a conference, but ultimately, more formal communication is necessary. This means presenting papers at conferences, preparing articles for a range of publications, and, for many, writing lengthy reports, monographs, and books. These tasks sometimes seem daunting, especially if you are at the beginning stages of a career. You might have seen the curriculum vitae (vita or c.v.) of your professor listing all of her or his publications and presented papers, thinking the whole time how much you struggled to get that ten-page paper done for the class you just took. Don't be too impressed; generally speaking, your professional life is long. That vita didn't appear overnight. If you develop certain skills and persevere, you'll find that your vita will look like that some day—and perhaps even better than your prof's!

A good place to start is by giving conference papers, the traditional way to inform colleagues about your work. Presenting papers also gives you a chance to discuss your ideas with other archaeologists before you put the work into print. However, even a paper starts with some writing: the abstract you send in to the conference to tell its organizers about your paper. Sadly but truly, an abstract is one of the most difficult kinds of writing there is.

ABSTRACTS

If you've been around archaeology very long, you'll know that learning how to construct an abstract is an essential skill. Everything seems to require them. Most conferences want an abstract, usually at some excruciatingly terse length. The conference program committee may use it to evaluate your paper for possible presentation. If they accept it, the abstract is put into the meeting program for colleagues to read to see whether they want to hear your paper or, barring that, to contact you later for a copy of the full paper.

Just about every CRM report short of the letter report seems to demand an abstract. If one might be a bit harsh, one starts to suspect that CRM bureaucrats don't like to read long CRM reports, so they have their contract managers demand abstracts of lengthier documents. Cynicism aside, abstracts can serve a more important function, even in the CRM world. Depending on the agency or state, abstracts of reports sometimes get published so that colleagues or other organizations can see key results from their research areas or jurisdictions. Most quality journals also demand abstracts of papers. In truth, there is such a glut of archaeological and other information being created that most scholars have learned how to skim or read abstracts to find out whether an article is worth their time or fits their research interests. Many online databases and abstract journals are now available, so abstracts are often published as stand-alone documents to aid researchers.

Abstracts are important! If you want someone to hear your paper or read your work, you need to pay careful attention to writing your abstract as you do to your full manuscript. Still, the whole idea of an abstract is tricky. You want to provide enough material to entice readers to hear your paper at a meeting or read the whole paper in a journal. At the same time, you don't want to give so much that they feel they have all your data, logic, and ideas fully encapsulated in the abstract so that they don't need to attend your presentation or read the full paper. Finding the right balance is often a dilemma.

Wherever the abstract is printed or whatever its length, its purpose is singular: to provide a summary of your work that can be quickly accessed and assessed by colleagues. As simple as it may seem, writing an abstract is no easy task, especially when you have to cram your whole project into as few as one hundred words! Sometimes simply knowing what an abstract is can help. An abstract should be a stand-alone statement that briefly conveys the essential information of a paper, article, CRM report, monograph, or book. In a short, nonrepetitive style, it presents the work's objectives, methods, results, and conclusions.

Abstracts are deceiving. They tend to appear in the first part of a paper, or they are usually sent to a conference program committee months before you give your paper. Even though they seem to come before anything else, the best abstracts are written after actually completing the full project. To do the best job, you really need to have finished your work before you can choose and summarize the essential information. Self-contained compactness is crucial, but if you try to write the abstract before the work is concluded, it can be a profoundly difficult task.

WHAT DO YOU PUT IN AN ABSTRACT?

STYLE GUIDES

What goes into an abstract may fully depend on the guidelines provided by the conference to which you are submitting the paper or the journal, publisher, or agency to which you are sending the manuscript. Some publications may have a required style for abstracts; guidelines for authors provided by a publisher or by organizers of specific conferences may provide specific instructions. The Society for American Archaeology, for example, asks for a two-hundred-word factual summary of the contents and conclusions of a submitted paper, with specific references to new information being presented and some indication of its relevance. The SAA specifically notes that the abstract should not be an introduction to the paper or an outline of it, with each section being reduced to a sentence. It also expressly asks authors to avoid passive voice.

TYPES OF ABSTRACTS

There are generally two types of abstracts, and they are not necessarily mutually exclusive. *Informative* abstracts summarize the entire report and give the reader an overview of the facts to be presented in detail in the paper. This type of abstract is normally of the sort used for conference papers, short reports, or relatively brief manuscripts such as that for a journal article. *Descriptive* abstracts are useful for longer documents such as monographs or CRM reports in which one cannot easily summarize all the findings of the project. It's a bit like the scope of work for a CRM project or a statement of purpose, describing a work's organization but not all of its content.

ABSTRACT STYLE

An abstract is no place for fancy style and convoluted prose. Writing needs to be straightforward and sparse. It doesn't need to have the same sentence structure or flow of the paper or report. Certainly, good grammar remains essential, but concise presentation of content is crucial.

WRITING THE ABSTRACT

Remember, in an abstract you are making a claim to knowledge. Thus, you succinctly need to tell the reader the boundaries of that knowledge, including time and space, as well as the limits to which you are willing to generalize from that knowledge. For archaeology this point is crucial, and many abstracts fail to make such boundaries clear. The abstract should precisely describe objectives, methods, results, and conclusions. Avoid any background information, don't make reference to the literature at all, and dump any thought of giving details of your methods or theoretical position.

December and Katz (1996) suggest that "writing an abstract involves boiling down the essence of a whole paper into a single paragraph that conveys as much new information as possible." They offer that

one way of writing an effective abstract is to start with a draft of the complete paper and do the following:
- Highlight the objective and the conclusions that are in the paper's introduction and the discussion.
- Bracket information in the methods section of the paper that contains keyword information.
- Highlight the results from the discussion or results section of the paper.
- Compile the above highlighted and bracketed information into a single paragraph.

- Condense the bracketed information into the key words and phrases that identify but do not explain the methods used.
- Delete extra words and phrases.
- Delete any background information.
- Rephrase the first sentence so that it starts off with the new information contained in the paper, rather than with the general topic. One way of doing this is to begin the first sentence with the phrase "this paper" or "this study."
- Revise the paragraph so that the abstract conveys the essential information.

Following this advice is not as easy as it might seem, but one does get better with practice. Remember, finally, that the abstract and the paper, monograph, or report are essentially parallel documents, but each must stand on its own.

A DOSE OF REALITY

Despite all the good advice out there about writing abstracts, most of you have gone to hear a particular paper at a meeting and found that it didn't sound much like the abstract published in the conference's abstracts volume. Many of you know exactly why that happens. Deadlines for submitting a presentation at a meeting often fall months before the conference. You might just have gotten out of the field or only be nearing completion of a complex bit of analysis. You haven't gotten anywhere close to being done with the manuscript. Still, you feel a need to give a paper on your work. What are you to do but make a guess about what you are actually going to find? You've probably heard all the good suggestions discussed already, but the odds are that you probably didn't have time to use them. Certainly, it's easier to write an abstract following this process when you've actually completed a manuscript, but when it comes to preparing an abstract for a conference paper, just about all of this advice goes out the window. If the abstract is due tomorrow, what should you do?

- Pay attention to some of the advice, at least.
- Give the boundaries of your work, temporally and spatially, unless the work is more generalizing.
- Be scrupulously honest, stating exactly how far along you are in your work, but it is fair to speculate what data analysis at this time seems to indicate.

- Avoid using jargon, even if you think such BS might snow the people reviewing your abstract or a reader; inappropriately used jargon just makes you look silly.
- Don't overextend your data, even if you think it might be supportive of certain hypotheses you propose.

Abstracts are vastly more important tools than most scholars realize. Most of us tend to think of them as a bother, but given their importance in convincing other scholars to read our work, we really should pay more attention to the way in which we construct them.

CONFERENCE PAPERS AND PUBLIC TALKS

One's first professional paper seems like such a rite of passage, remembered for the rest of your career. (If you're lucky, you'll be the only one who remembers it!) Giving professional presentations and papers is a professional obligation, used to inform colleagues about our research and giving them a chance to provide criticism. Publication in print and on the web provides other mechanisms for feedback, but having a group of colleagues together at one time provides a compelling dynamic. Giving talks is part of our accountability to the public, an ethical obligation.

WHY WE GIVE PAPERS AND PRESENTATIONS

The real reasons we give conference papers or public talks are easy to forget. In the crush of academic life, we get pushed to present papers in order to have our way to a conference paid or to build our credentials. In the CRM world, an agency's scope of work may require you to give a professional presentation to showcase its project. Sometimes in university life, you are asked to give presentations as part of a well-defined service obligation. These mask the real reason for presentations.

More than anything, conference papers are for the exchange of information with colleagues. It's important to have your peers know about your work and to swap ideas with you based on their own experiences on similar subjects. Presentations to groups not made up of colleagues are service, a way to pay archaeology's bills, so to speak, by letting them know what we learn from the tax or foundation dollars we spend. For all the energy spent on preparing for the papers and talks, most of us tend to forget this. Whatever the politics of conferences, whatever the possibilities of getting shot down by a colleague or a heckler, remember why you give a paper. The idea is to get your data, thoughts, and logic into a larger arena than that between your ears or around the company coffeepot!

GLOSSOPHOBIA

If you've never given a paper before, the process might seem daunting or the fear overwhelming. Your anxiety probably starts with *glossophobia*, the fear of speaking in front of an audience. Public speaking is a fear shared by many people (more than 40 percent). In fact, according to the *People's Almanac Book of Lists*, the fear of speaking in public is the number one fear of all fears, while the fear of dying is a mere number seven! The truth, however, is that speaking in public probably won't kill you. You need to learn to deal with the fear, or you simply will not do all that well in archaeology. Hiding with your nose in an excavation unit or at the end of a caliper in a lab just won't work.

You undoubtedly have had a number of opportunities to learn and practice public speaking, but if you are like most, you probably found ways to avoid it. As an undergraduate, you probably had to take a required speech class but, like lots of students, put it off until the last semester of your final year (along with the math requirement?). In graduate training, you might have had ample opportunity to report your findings in a seminar class, but perhaps you avoided certain seminars entirely because you were afraid to present findings in class. If your glossophobia is that great, you probably need some professional help to overcome the fear, but if your fear is average, there are a lot of things you can do to control anxiety.

The single most important piece of advice is that you prepare yourself well. This tip might seem obvious, but in the crunch of time, most of us don't take into account what preparation means and leave scant time for it. You need to do more than just read your paper over a few times. Good advice on overcoming your anxiety and on how to prepare can be found all over the Internet and on many bookshelves, but some of the best comes from Toastmasters International, a fine organization dedicated to helping people become better public speakers. They have chapters in most areas, many of them on college and university campuses. You can get tips on speaking and experience, as well as "safe" criticism from them. Their website (www.toastmasters.org/tips.htm) has excellent tips for preparing yourself.

TIPS AND REALITIES

The Toastmasters International tips and others like them are all fine, but the reality of public presentation is a different thing altogether. Most tips are good and will help you, but some are crucial to success as a speaker.

KNOW THE ROOM

During a two-year stint as a National Lecturer for Sigma Xi, the Scientific Research Society, I gave more than thirty lectures. I spoke in everything from a bare classroom with a slide projector on the arm of a student desk to fancy lecture halls where the podium was as well equipped as the bridge of the *Starship Enterprise*. Usually I was afforded a chance to check out the room, something I'd advise every time and something I do at every conference before I give a paper. You just don't know what you will find!

In some ways, I'd say that you also owe this level of acquaintance with the room to your audience. They have a right to see and hear you, or at least to expect you to be prepared (although some problems may just be out of your control). Consider the following:

- If possible, ask someone else to come with you, and have them listen to you speak in the room.
- If the room is so large that a microphone is needed, be sure that you know how to use it. How far from the mike can you lean or move and still have it pick up your voice? If you have a lavaliere microphone, how far can you move around on the cable without strangling yourself or tripping over it? If you have a radio microphone, consider yourself lucky!
- How do your visuals look at a distance? Check their size from different spots in the room, so that you can describe them better if graphics are too small.
- Learn how the slide projector works, and run through your slides if there is time.
- See whether there is a pointer, water, or other things you might need.

If nothing else, by checking these things out you'll at least feel comfortable, but doing so may also help you avoid disaster during your talk.

KNOW YOUR AUDIENCE

Before you speak somewhere, always find out the nature of the audience. If you haven't been told, ask! Based on your assessment of audience background, your entire tone, style of presentation, and parts of the content may need to be varied. For an audience of professional colleagues, you have a right to expect that they will at least know most of the jargon. Certainly, your professional paper can and should be different from that given to the local archaeological society. You should be smart enough to recognize audience differences and prepare for them. If the presentation is something you might give several times, you can actually prepare talks with different slides and text for different audiences. Though doing so takes a bit of extra work, it's worth it.

KNOW YOUR MATERIAL

Nothing should give you confidence so much as the fact that you know your material better than anyone else, but that's not all there is to it. The real trick is practice. Having your logic of presentation and any visual materials well prepared is the starting place, but real confidence in your material comes from practice. You can only feel confident if you've gone through the presentation enough that you don't really need to worry about the material. You know what argument is next, you know what slide follows the one on the screen and that it is not upside down, and you know how an audience might react to what you show or say. Nothing can throw you.

Knowing your material will help you succeed in a way that more archaeologists giving conference papers should remember: Don't read your paper; give it! Nothing is more deadly than a person reading a paper. Attend any conference, and you'll hear many read papers. Unless the presenter is very skilled, has used a speaking style, and has practiced carefully, reading a paper can be a disaster. Most people don't write like they speak; they go long, and the audience can't follow complex spoken arguments because they don't have time to think about them like they have when they read. Usually, you are better off having an outline to speak from or, as many do, using your illustrations as your outline. If you are nervous and need a "crutch," you might have a full copy with you in case you get lost, but do your best to avoid using it.

When you first start giving talks or lectures, being nervous is natural, but you can even prepare for that. I require that my teaching assistants give a lecture in my classes so that they can get a feel for what that situation is like. Most are justifiably terrified at their first lecture. I always tell them to prepare just about twice as much material as they think they'll need because with their nervousness, they'll rush through it. After you calm down, you can always cut material if you are going long, but if you don't have enough, it can be pretty difficult to wing your way through another fifteen minutes.

The more you practice, the more you can pay attention to other elements of your presentation. You can get to a point where it's almost like an out-of-body experience. You know the material so well and are so practiced that you can almost step outside yourself to objectively assess how you are doing. You can pay attention to the "acting" part of public speaking. Most important, you can pay attention to your audience and how they are responding to what you're saying, using the feedback to adjust pace, explain terms better, and assess their understanding. Believe it or not, you can actually enjoy lecturing to large groups.

Obviously, delivering conference papers is different but nonetheless requires detailed preparation. If you are a student, ask your professor whether there are opportunities for you to give a paper. You might be able to tailor it to an audience of advanced students, filling in for your professor for a class period. Perhaps a department seminar is being held where you can try out your paper. Wouldn't you rather bomb in front of your fellow graduate students and faculty members than at a professional meeting? If there aren't adequate departmental opportunities, you can organize graduate student brown-bag lunches where you can try out your talk. If nothing else, find a friend or two so that you can practice; do ask for their honest feedback. If you are a young professional in a nonacademic setting, perhaps you can arrange a small Friday afternoon seminar for your CRM firm. Again, if nothing else, try to arrange for a few friends or colleagues to hear you give the talk aloud.

ANSWERING QUESTIONS

Most talks you give will probably generate questions. At conferences, questions are usually limited by the amount of time available or the structure of the session. Luncheon talks may be limited by the amount of time the audience has. Other talks may be open-ended for questions. You rarely know what kinds of questions will come out of a talk, but if you've given a talk often, you can usually predict some of them. If you are speaking on something controversial, be prepared for challenging questions, but don't be afraid of them. After all, you wouldn't be speaking on the topic if you didn't have evidence or some level of confidence. If you are speaking to a class or audience of non-specialists, the questions can be lots of fun (though eventually you will have a heckler who wants you to justify the cost of a dig or some such silliness). When your talk affords an opportunity for questions, remember these tips:

- Relax and listen carefully to the question.
- Allow questions during the talk itself if you are comfortable with that structure.
- Ask for clarification if you couldn't hear or didn't understand the question.
- If the question is long and complicated, try to break it up into parts.
- Some people ask questions that are actually statements, not requiring an answer, so don't worry about the answer, and don't be afraid to challenge them gently if they are off target.
- If someone tries to dominate or consistently challenge you, tell him or her you will be happy to deal with the question afterward, allowing others a chance to ask questions.
- Show respect for every person who asks a question, even if the question is poorly phrased. Really stupid questions are rare, but many are badly asked.
- If you don't know the answer, don't be afraid to say you don't know!

Don't be afraid to have some fun with questions. In fact, a general rule suggests that the more questions asked, the better your talk was. The more practice you get, the easier it is to handle questions. Believe it or not, you'll actually start to enjoy the tough ones.

GAINING EXPERIENCE: FINDING OPPORTUNITIES TO SPEAK

If you haven't done much public speaking, start small with your talks. Undergraduates can give papers and presentations at low-key meetings such as at a chapter or state meeting for an archaeological society or the anthropology section of the state Academy of Sciences at its annual meeting. These venues usually have supportive people, sometimes with classmates or people from the archaeology lab where you work. You'll be nervous but fine.

Then move up. Find a larger but friendly place to give a paper and gain experience. Some regional meetings such as the Plains Conference or the Midwest Archaeological Conference have reputations as being places where graduate students give their first professional papers. If you are confident, then why not go for one of the national meetings, such as those of the SAA or the American Anthropological Association? (See sidebar 8.1 for some tips on presenting at the SAA annual conference and sidebar 8.2 for pointers on using graphics.) You might consider teaming yourself with another student or one of your professors on a joint paper where you only give part of it and are supported by a more experienced speaker.

There are also lots of local places to get experience. Many service organizations are constantly in need of luncheon or banquet speakers.

8.1. HELPFUL HINTS ON PRESENTING A PAPER AT THE ANNUAL MEETING OF THE SOCIETY FOR AMERICAN ARCHAEOLOGY (1997, REVISED 1999)

A. Before the Meeting

1. Read your paper a number of times aloud to make sure it is within the 15 minute maximum. (Printed out in 12 pt. font, a 15-minute presentation consumes 5 double-spaced pages. No more than 14–15 slides should accompany your presentation.)
2. Once you are happy with your paper, do a "dress" rehearsal with slides for an audience. Make sure that you are still within the 15-minute time limit. Ask for criticism and revise if necessary. Ideally, your presentation should be 14 minutes long.
3. If your illustrations contain text or graphics, make sure that they can be read from the back of a large room. Captions on figures and graphs should be in a larger font than you would use for publication, i.e., 21 pt. or larger. A slide should only remain on the screen for as long as it is relevant to what you are saying. You can leave gaps in the slides so that the audience concentrates on you and not an irrelevant illustration.
4. Print your paper in a large font (e.g. 16 pt.), so that you can easily read it in dim light. Mark clearly on the paper when a slide is to be shown. (If you intend to discuss the illustration, make sure that you have included

The sandwich buffet and rubber chicken circuit for Lions Club, Optimists, and assorted other service groups is excellent. One way to put yourself on this circuit is to register with your university's speakers bureau if it has one. Schoolteachers also look for specialists to speak to their classes. If you have a local anthropology or natural history museum, you might inquire whether it needs docents or tour guides. This role can get monotonous after your fifteenth tour, but it will give your a chance to get comfortable in front of different sorts of groups and used to answering insightful and inane questions.

Giving these talks gives you an early start in returning something of our profession to the general public. The situation is not too difficult, and audiences truly are grateful to you. Speaking to the public or your peers is an important part of what an archaeologist does, but something that rarely comes automatically to anyone. To become a proficient speaker requires preparation and lots of practice.

the discussion in the timing of your paper. To be sure about this, write down what you want to say about the illustration.)
5. Put your slides in a tray to bring to the meeting (SAA does not supply slide trays). Keep your paper, illustrations, and presentation attire with you on the airplane. Don't allow your presentation to suffer just because your luggage was lost!
6. You will be asked by interested scholars for a copy of your paper. Prepare distribution copies, which might be copies of the paper from which your presentation was abstracted.

B. At the Meeting

1. As soon as you register, check the date and time of your paper. It may have changed from the schedule published in the preliminary program.
2. Make sure you know in which room you will be presenting your paper.
3. Visit the room before your symposium or session begins. Check that your slides will show up on the screen properly. Make sure you know how the projector controls work.
4. Arrive at your symposium 15 minutes early. Introduce yourself to the chair. Talk to the volunteer running the projector and lights. Explain what sort of lighting you would like.
5. Smile!

8.2. SOCIETY FOR AMERICAN ARCHAEOLOGY GRAPHIC PRESENTATION TIPS

Dos

Use landscape orientation; screens at most presentation forums are designed for landscape format slides.

Enhance the readability of text by using LARGE (24 pt or better) font size.

Use lower and upper case letters (your eye has more "topographic" information to use than with block letters).

Use line weight, style, symbol, etc. to convey important information.

Keep it simple.

Choose fonts with serif.

Check for misspellings.

Maintain consistency in images, legends, colors, between slides.

Check graphic margins for slides; most graphics packages have a media format default set for the monitor or for paper.

Don'ts

Use profile [portrait] orientation; the tops or bottoms of slides will likely not be projected onto the screens.

Use small (less than 24 pt) font size; there is no excuse for "You probably can't read this, but. . . ."

Overuse of block letters; use them with the maximum size font on the graphic.

Use red and green on same slide (40% of men cannot distinguish between the two).

Use complex slides (break down ideas).

Use a sans serif font.

Substitute paper graphic for slide graphic; paper and slide presentations have different audiences and environments, and therefore require different designs.

Use 3D graphics when 2D will suffice.*

Presentation Tip

Slide Presentations: Figure on using one (1) slide per minute of presentation. The human mind cannot take in complex graphical Information at a rate faster than this.

Reference

Tufte, Edward R.
1983 *The Visual Display of Quantitative Information.* Graphics Press, Cheshire, CT.

*Edward Tufte and other experts in data communication argue that our eyes are very good at interpreting 3D forms and often do so in unintended ways. Therefore, the possibility of miscommunication is greater here. You should closely inspect 3D graphs; they are not what they seem.

DEVELOP SOME "CANNED" TALKS

If you spend time developing a good talk or lecture for the general public, or in some cases even a professional lecture, spend time to package or "can" it. Think carefully about what worked and what didn't, then make appropriate changes. Be certain to keep any slides together along with any other support materials you need. You'd be surprised how many people are just so relieved to have a talk done that they don't even think about the possibility of giving it again. They take the slides out of the slide tray and forget about the talk, and then they later regret that they didn't just leave the slides in the tray.

If the talk was successful and the slides are laboratory or office property, get permission to have them copied so that you have a set. The cost of a slide tray and copies of even thirty or so slides is rather small compared to the time you might need to reconstruct the whole talk. You can even package it to give to different kinds or levels of audiences. If the opportunity to give a lecture a second or third time comes up, you'll be very glad you canned the lecture.

POSTER PAPERS?
HOW TO DECIDE AND HOW TO DELIVER

For academic conferences, poster papers have almost become a necessity to allow the conference program committee to squeeze in several more presentations. Cynicism suggests that allowing for more presenters is the primary reason poster papers came into existence, but posters actually are a fine idea. The format is straightforward. With posters grouped in common themes (methodological, topical, geographic area, etc.), presenters come to a room set aside for the poster papers. The themes change on a schedule like that for regular paper sessions, but poster sessions usually allow at least an hour or more per session for posters to be viewed. The presenter sets up the poster and is available for questions as viewers come by. The posters appear on standard-size poster boards, often four by eight feet. Sometimes the boards will be on a table so that a presenter can lay out printed copies of the paper text, business cards, artifacts, and other objects as they need them. At other times, the poster boards are stand-alone, with no table space.

The benefits of poster papers are many. The most important benefits are that viewers can take more time to digest the paper and to ask questions. The fifteen minutes allowed for most oral papers is usually not enough time, and presenters tend to rush through their talk or simply read a written paper. Graphics are sometimes ill chosen for viewers, with almost no time allowed for them to digest the content. Unless the session is well planned to include questions and well chaired to keep things on schedule, there is almost never time for them until after the session ends. Poster sessions usually allow for more interchange between presenter and viewer. An added benefit for some is that there is no public performance and little need to worry about speaking in public. Most interaction is one-on-one or in very small groups.

Poster sessions do have some drawbacks. For some strange reason, many colleagues think that poster papers are less important than oral papers. Depending on your situation, you may need to forego posters for traditional presentation, especially if you are on a tenure and promotion track. You may not get as large an audience as traditional sessions provide. Much of this depends on where organizers place the poster session. At a recent Plains/Midwest joint conference, the posters were in the lobby area of the conference center, a terrific location through which everyone passed several times a day. At the recent American Anthropological Association (AAA) meeting, posters were right by the book exhibit area, also a good location. If posters get shoved into a room out of the way, it can be the kiss of death for having your work seen. The very best location may be near where foods for session breaks get placed. (Conference organizers, take note of all this!)

All the problems aside, with the poster paper format you may get a more attentive, interested audience able to spend more time looking at your work. You can answer individual questions and make useful contacts, usually in a less time-stressed setting. Although one-on-one contact is terrific, one drawback is that you will constantly repeat the same information as your audience changes.

HOW DO YOU PUT TOGETHER A GOOD POSTER PAPER?

What makes for a good poster paper? Just as with a traditional delivery, you first need a good paper! However, poster papers are essentially show-and-tell. Limit the amount of information directly on the poster. As with museum exhibits, your poster will compete for attention with other posters in the room. Thus, you cannot—no, *must not*—try to put the whole paper up on the poster. People usually won't spend the time reading all your text. A recent trend in poster sessions has been toward doing just that. Using Adobe PageMaker or some other layout program, many have taken to putting all their text and graphics on a single large, printed poster. These look really slick but are almost impossible to work your way through as a reader, especially if the poster session is crowded. Too many try to cram thirty pages of text onto a poster along with all their graphics. This utterly defeats the purpose of poster papers, whose strength is in providing conclusions and graphics. In terms of presenting information, some of the most effective posters look the least slick.

You can still be slick, but don't overwhelm the viewer with lots of complex text or graphics. One effective approach is to do the paper as a series of Power Point or other presentation software slides. With these, you can print out color pages and simply tack them on the board. They also allow for a great deal of flexibility with different poster board setups. Woe to the archaeologist who has gone to great effort and expense to print out a three-foot by four-foot color poster only to find that he doesn't have that much space or has a trifold poster setup! One paper by a senior archaeologist at the recent AAA was little more than photographs of people, artifacts, and excavations relating to the historical Colorado Coal Wars along with small amounts of text, all thumbtacked to the poster board. The poster was stark and minimalist, almost antislick, but still very effective. That archaeologist knew something special about how to do posters!

Posters work best with graphical information, so you should try to determine whether the core of your paper could best be presented graphically. Then present the core, not all the information and logic of the paper. Put up only key points of logic and conclusions as text, but emphasize the graphics. You can have copies of the whole paper with you or on the table to give to those who are really interested. If you have lots of statistics and charts that wouldn't show well in a traditional paper and whose presentation is vital to your conclusions, a poster may be ideal. On the other hand, if you have a largely theoretical paper, with few graphics, stick with traditional papers. If you have lots of artifact photos or actual artifacts to lay out, a poster is again ideal. If you have table space for actual artifacts, presenting them there can be effective. Sadly, however, if you display artifacts, you do need to worry about theft, even among colleagues. If you use them, be there with them all the time, and pay attention.

If you are showing a specialized computer program, such as a website or CD-ROM, poster sessions are also ideal, with one drawback. If you draw a crowd, no more than a few people at a time can see the screen. On the other hand, people can actually see or use the product with fewer constraints on time. However, you need to be sure there are electrical outlets, Internet connections, and access to other needed computer connections.

For a good poster paper, do the following:

1. Write a good paper.
2. Decide whether to do the poster. To do so:
   - Decide whether the information can be well presented graphically. If it would be difficult, do a traditional paper.
   - Find out from the organizers how long the posters will be up and where they will be shown at the conference.
3. Select four or so key points to emphasize on your poster if they can presented graphically.
4. Choose graphics wisely to demonstrate the points but also to catch the eye of viewers.
5. Find out ahead of time what the organizers will provide. This includes:
   - the size of poster space;
   - the nature of the poster board (a wall, a flat bulletin board, a trifold, table space);
   - pins, tape, and other accessories including computer capabilities.

   If you wish to bring your own setup, let the organizers know so they can tell whether it is feasible. Conference facilities may not allow it.
6. Organize your information within the constraints of the poster setup.
7. You may also wish to consider having business cards, a summary handout with contact information or website addresses where people can see the whole paper, and a few copies of the whole paper for those who might like more information or who wish to contact you.

If you are considering a poster paper, two articles in the *SAA Bulletin* have addressed how to construct good poster papers and offer a range of tips (Neiman 1994; Baxter 1996). Neiman provides some detailed how-to advice. Baxter's (1996:9,31) article is especially useful. She provides a list of criteria for judging poster paper quality at the

SAA meetings (see sidebar 8.3) developed by David Anderson, a former SAA Annual Meeting program chair and a judge for poster sessions at several SAA meeting. She also relates some tips from Alanah Woody who won the SAA Student Poster Award in 1994. Many of these are the same as discussed earlier but are worth repeating. She notes:

- Preparing a poster is an expensive venture. Matte board, photo enlargements, and other graphic materials can add up quickly!
- Have hard copies of a "real" publishable paper on hand to go with your poster, complete with chaining arguments, citations, and a bibliography. Separate bibliographies and business cards are also good ideas.
- Posters are not the same as paper. You do not have space to support every argument. Use your poster to spark enough interest so people will ask for a copy of your paper.
- Read how-to articles about creating an effective poster, but also add your own touches to make your poster unique and noteworthy.

Baxter makes another excellent suggestion. If you've gone to all the trouble and expense of preparing a poster, she suggests that you recycle it. In one sense, a poster is like a small museum exhibit. If the poster is well done, it's probably worth showing again. Perhaps it can

8.3. JUDGING A GOOD POSTER

Subject matter: A great site or topic makes a great poster!
Production values: Legible text, colorful artwork, and effective arrangement are essential for a poster.
Clarity: Is the technical argument well presented? Is the flow of information logical and easy to follow?
Absorbable level of detail: Do not try to squeeze in too much information by using small type or presenting too many graphics.
First impressions are critical: Effective posters have a "hook" either in the subject matter or in its presentation.
Cleverness and originality of presentation: Posters that are new or unique and effective in presenting information will stand out.
(From David Anderson, in Baxter 1996:31.)

be put up in your lab area, much as the Office of the State Archaeologist of Iowa does. If the subject matter is not too esoteric, the poster might go well as a temporary exhibit in a small museum on your campus, town, or county.

The AAA website (www.aaanet.org/mtgs/poster.htm) also provides a substantial set of suggestions for preparing poster papers. Although the materials give AAA-specific guidelines, the page asks excellent questions everyone giving a poster paper should consider. It also contains a short bibliography of materials from other fields about poster papers.

ELECTRONIC SESSIONS

A recent trend allowed by the World Wide Web is to put whole conference sessions on the Internet. As with poster papers, part of the reason for doing this is to allow for more papers in conferences, but the trend also has other benefits. One problem with traditionally delivered papers, and even poster papers, is that the presenters must summarize what they've done to meet time or space constraints. Likewise, viewers rarely have much time to consider what they've heard or seen. With electronic sessions, full papers with a wide range of illustrative materials can be put on the web well ahead of the conference. All session participants and possible attendees can read the papers and have time to think about them. At the actual conference, the papers are briefly summarized, and all the remaining time can be spent on discussing them among the participants and attendees. This approach may entail a more efficient use of time, but it has some drawbacks.

Participants do have to provide a full draft version of their paper ahead of time. If procrastinators are participating in the session, as they always seem to, papers may still come in late or in poor shape. If you are a procrastinator, don't offer to participate in an electronic session! Someone also has to be able to put the papers up on the web. This is really not big problem, but it does take time, and one does need to have access to web space.

Some participants are paranoid about having their work on the web, either because they feel embarrassed at others seeing their work or because they are worried about people stealing their ideas. Session materials can be password protected, but this may limit the audience. If you fit these definitions of paranoid, the electronic session is probably not for you! The conference organizers must also list the session as part of the regular conference sessions and provide the web address to possible attendees well ahead of time. If they don't, no one but participants will have a chance to preview the papers and may not wish to attend the session.

On the whole, the electronic approach is a new one, with organizations such as the SAA only just trying it out. Having organized my first such session for the 2001 SAA meetings, I can now make several observations about how it went. On the plus side, the discussion was fantastic. One audience member e-mailed me about how she enjoyed not being read or lectured to and having a real opportunity for substantive discussion. Many of the attendees participated, and when asked how they liked the session, they were uniform in praise of the format. The presenters agreed that the discussion was excellent and that their own anxieties about being there were dramatically lower than when giving a paper. On the minus side, when I asked the audience how many had read the papers ahead, only five had. When I asked how many even knew of the session before getting to the meetings, only six said they had. Clearly, the format is useful, but there are lots of bugs to work out—and if you are a session organizer, you'll find there are sometimes more than you'd like.

ORGANIZING AND CHAIRING A SESSION

Sometime in your career you will find a compelling subject on which you are doing research and know that others are doing similar research. You may also be part of a collaborative CRM project team, perhaps even its director, and will realize that your team needs to present its findings. On a sad occasion—when a colleague or mentor has died, for example—you may wish to assemble former students and colleagues to memorialize the individual. For a more joyful occasion, you may wish to assemble colleagues and students to honor the contributions and retirement of a colleague or mentor in a session that sometimes results in a written collection called a *festschrift*. Whatever the situation, you will need to organize the colleagues around a central theme and propose the theme and session for a meeting that eventually will get turned into an edited volume.

Doing so may be no small feat, or it may be little effort at all, mostly depending on your colleagues. Usually colleagues feel honored to be invited to present a paper in a session, although they may eventually complain about deadlines or your heavy-handed nagging. Memorials and festschrifts may have no central theme except the person around whom the session gets organized. Thematic sessions often require more organization.

Planning for any session needs to begin well ahead of the meeting dates, in fact, well ahead of the submission deadlines for meetings. Most regional meetings have deadlines closer to the actual meetings than do national meetings, but in both cases submission of a complete session package may be eight to twelve months ahead of the meetings. This allows organizers time to arrange sessions and rooms. Good session planning might allow at least two to three months ahead of the deadline, but even that may be pushing it.

Once you have a theme for a meeting, you should choose an appropriate venue. Festschrift and memorial sessions are often more appropriate for regional or small national meetings unless the honoree is/was a nationally recognized figure in archaeology. In some ways, so are sessions surrounding a single site unless the site has national or international significance. Thematic sessions will do for most meetings. If you have an idea for a thematic meeting but don't always know who might be working on the topic, you may wish to include a note about the planned session in regional or national newsletters; some even have "cooperation" columns. You can also send out e-mails to colleagues you know who are working on the topic or who may have students or other colleagues who are doing so. With contacts made, you can begin to assemble the session.

Most organizations have very strict structures for submission of sessions. Be sure to get all the necessary forms for the participants and distribute them in plenty of time for submission by the deadlines. Forms usually come in printed flyers mailed out to organization members or are now available on many organizations' websites. National organizations usually demand submission of an entire session packet. The packet usually consists of a session abstract, the forms of each of the participants, and, more and more often, advanced registration materials and fees for all session participants. All this may sound easy, but getting participants to get materials in on time, submitting their abstracts in the proper form (assuming there is a standard form), or paying their registration fees in advance often takes more nagging than you might imagine!

As you prepare to submit the session, read the abstracts over carefully. Try to find commonalties that will allow you to order the papers for the session. Look for common ideas that may link papers, and then play with different orderings. Oddly enough, this is almost like doing the lineup for a baseball game. You need something to gain the audience's attention early, so you may want to put "bigger names" near the start, followed by the more esoteric or weaker papers in the middle, and then, near the end, the more theoretical or synthetic papers, even another "bigger name." This can be followed by discussants who are chosen for their expertise or ability to summarize and critique.

After you submit the session, and assuming the organization accepts it, you need to inform all session members that the session is moving ahead. You will need to set a deadline for submission of the session papers to you, especially if you have one or more discussants, individuals who critique the papers or provide a synthesis of the session. These individuals need to see the papers ahead of time to make appropriate comments. In truth, all the papers making it to the discussant in time to digest them before the session is a rarity, and one of great joy for the discussant. This accomplishment often takes genuine harassment of participants, but it will make for a better session. Having been a discussant many times, I know how difficult it is to listen to a paper and have to invent sage comments just from listening to a hastily prepared and badly delivered paper! One of my more jovial colleagues has even taken to giving cute prizes for people who get papers in on time and for those who don't. Believe me, you don't want one of his prizes for those who don't get papers in on time.

A bit before the session, you would be wise to contact the presenters to see whether any unusual problems or needs have popped up. Even though abstract and session submission forms ask what presentation equipment, such as slide projectors, are needed, some presenters insist on special equipment, such as a computer with Internet connections and a projector. These may or may not be possible for the organizations, but you can do the presenter the courtesy of checking. You should also tell the presenters to assemble at a particular time and place before the session to introduce themselves to you. If this isn't possible, try to leave them your hotel number at the information center many conferences have, and ask them at least to call to say they have arrived. Nothing is more nerve-wracking than waiting to see whether your presenters have arrived when the session is about to start. If you can't meet before the session, ask them to be certain they introduce themselves to you before the session starts, particularly if you don't know them well.

If you organized the session, plan on the first paper being your own, or plan for a short introduction of the session topic to an audience that may not be fully aware of what the session is about. During the session, your job will be to introduce the speakers, so you may wish to ask them to submit a very brief biography for your introduction.

The biggest problem at sessions is time. Many speakers do very well at staying within allotted times, but others are a disaster! You certainly need to bring a watch or timer of some sort. You may wish to instruct the speakers on how you will notify them of the time. Some session chairs hold up small sheets of paper with the amount of time left: "ten minutes," "five minutes," "one minute," "stop." Be judicious in the use of such papers because they can interrupt a speaker who is well rehearsed and organized to the extent that the talk takes more time should she lose her place. On the other hand, unless you have had a speaker drop out, you may need to be strict about cutting off a speaker. Don't be embarrassed about it; just do it! A speaker going over time limits takes time from other speakers, limits any time for discussion, and may throw off a session following yours, if scheduling is tight.

FROM GIVING A PAPER TO DISCUSSING A SESSION

If you are a session organizer, you may wish to find an individual who can help you tie the content of all the papers together. If your session is a memorial or festschrift, you may wish to have someone present an overview of the honoree's contributions. This should usually be someone who has been a colleague or a former student. You might ask for some reminiscences as well as a few comments about each paper. For a thematic or site-centered session, you should choose discussants who are extremely knowledgeable about the topic, whose work is respected, and who are capable of synthesizing information quickly.

To be asked to be a discussant is both an honor and a chore. If you agree to be a discussant, your own sins will come back to haunt you! You'll curse the presenters who never get papers to you and recall every time you never got your paper to the discussant ahead of time. There are several approaches to being a discussant. If you are a rare individual who can "wing it" upon hearing a group of papers, you can simply listen and then get up and give cogent comments. Most of us are not that adept, so a better approach is to take what papers have come in, read them a couple of times, and then devise a general set of comments into which additional papers will probably fit.

As you sit in the session, listen for changes that speakers who submitted advanced papers might have made. Listen carefully to those you've not read. Take notes on each, but not too many to pull together. As you listen to the last paper, pull things together, and pray that if there is more than one discussant, you are not the first! Being last can have drawbacks, however, in that others may say all the things you wanted to say. In any event, thank the session organizers and paper presenters briefly; then open with general comments, followed by something about each paper. You don't have much time, so you must hit only key points, both good and bad, about each. You do not necessarily need to address each paper in order, though doing so may be easier. You can end with more general comments about the subject or any general issues you'd like to raise regarding the subject. This can serve as a spark to urge further research or address particular questions or concerns about the subject.

As a discussant, you have a certain degree of power. If everyone in the group is senior and the subject is of import to archaeology, you may have been chosen because the organizer(s) wanted you to be controversial. Senior people are very capable of defending themselves, so you need not worry about offending. However, in my own experience, I can't say that I've heard a paper yet without some redemptive qualities. If the participants are early in their careers or even in the middle, what you say can have a profound influence on their self-image. You need to be honest in your criticisms, and you don't need to give false praise, but you should avoid attacking the speaker. Some individuals let power and reputation go to their heads, even "counting coup" on graduate students when discussing a paper. No one likes to be humiliated!

Such behavior is unfortunate, at best. If you can find good qualities in the paper, try to balance gentle criticism with faint praise, or don't say anything. If you find serious fault, you can approach the individual after the session, buy him a cup of coffee or a beer, and offer more direct criticism and even assistance in fixing problems.

Another problem for discussants is to heap praise on some papers while saying nothing about others, which sends a message that the latter are not worth your time. If you can, try to say something about each paper unless it is so bad that it needs more private discussion. If there is more than one discussant, you might arrange to chat with your counterparts ahead of time and agree to concentrate on certain papers so each gets some level of attention. If you must use being a discussant as a bully pulpit, steer clear of comments that can be seen as ad hominem attacks or as self-serving. The true role of a discussant is to help improve the papers by providing feedback with suggestions for research, clarifying logic or arguments, and providing a synthesis of key ideas from the session. In a sense, it is "instant" peer review, aimed at improving the product.

CONCLUSION

Papers presented at conferences are an important way of disseminating information to colleagues, but the audience is relatively small, even compared to the number of readers of state or regional journals. Giving a conference paper should not be considered an end in itself, unless of course, you are just trying to pry travel money out of the hands of your company's CEO or your dean! Even then, conferences are so cluttered with papers that if getting travel money is the only reason to give a paper, you should do yourself and colleagues a favor and at least make it a poster or electronic symposium presentation.

The real reasons for conference papers are to let colleagues know what you are doing, to exchange ideas on research, and to get feedback on your work. Putting the paper into writing should be a more important goal than giving conference papers. Your work can be read by more people and will have a greater chance of having an impact on the profession. This is the subject of chapter 9.

9

FROM PRESENTED TO PRINTED

Archaeologists have to do lots of writing. We have our day-to-day chores, from the e-mails and memos we send colleagues to proposals to agencies we hope will fund our next project. Some of these find their way into our presentations of the past, so we need to spend time doing them well. You may not worry about an e-mail sent to a colleague explaining your views about Woodland tradition taxonomy, but you might find your colleague asking for permission to quote your statement in an article. Your outline of a research design in a proposal may end up as part of a chapter in a CRM report.

The materials in this chapter, however, are geared toward the kinds of formal presentations of the past that might end up in print. Because much of this series is aimed at CRM practitioners, we'll start with CRM reports, which are specific to projects prepared for agencies, the major product of the vast majority of research money spent on archaeology. They are often heavily peer reviewed but are called a "gray literature" because they usually don't have a wide distribution. Relatively short works, journal articles, and newsletters are periodical or serial literature produced by professional organizations or other publishers. Books and monographs are longer treatments of a subject produced by a variety of publishers and may be collections of shorter chapters. These printed forms are linked by common issues of peer review and editing, which we'll consider at some length.

CRM REPORTS

Cultural resource management reports have become the core of data production in archaeology. Many projects are not CRM based, but the majority of basic fieldwork no longer comes from private or academic research programs. CRM reports are so variable in form that it is difficult to discuss them in a general sense, but some issues are common in the preparation of most reports.

The initial element of concern is that the report should meet the requirements of the organization contracting with you for the work. After all, it's paying for the work. Some agencies, especially if they are federal, may have particular requirements in terms of formats and perhaps even style guides. You should be certain before you start any writing that you know and understand these requirements. Doing so may save you lots of rewriting time! Don't waste time trying to convince a contracting agency to do things your way instead of theirs, unless what they ask violates professional and personal ethics. Some things, such as the spelling of *archeology* without the *a*, instead of *archaeology* with it, are just not worth worrying about!

As important as agency contract requirements are any standards for reports developed by organizations such as the State Historic Preservation Office (SHPO), state archaeologist, or professional associations. These may be fairly detailed, even to the kind and size of maps or illustrations to be included. Some SHPOs allow letter reports for negative findings so long as there is enough detail for them to make an assessment of the quality of work. Others may require a more complete report, even when you find nothing.

The main elements of any CRM report these:

- A statement of the project area, in terms of both planned land disturbance and archaeological coverage
- A section on the culture history of the project area in terms of what might be expected concerning site types and cultures and how what might be found is connected to the state plan for cultural resources
- Field methods used
- A section on the geomorphology and soils of an area and how your project assessed possible buried sites
- Sites and materials recovered
- An assessment of the archaeological materials in terms of significance regarding the National Register of Historic Places

- Any recommendations you have regarding cultural resources within the project area

Besides meeting these elements of content or format, you should also pay careful attention to the scope of work under which you were acting, as well as any proposal you submitted regarding the project. Be certain that you address every important aspect of both documents. Doing so will provide both the contracting agency and the SHPO with ways of seeing that the required work got done.

THE PROBLEM OF BOILERPLATES

Boilerplates are documents or parts of documents prepared ahead of time and then worked into a report. The idea is to save you from constantly having to rewrite the same part of a document many times. For example, many organizations have prepared boilerplate sections about the culture history of an area or about the geomorphology of a region. Boilerplates are meant to be altered to meet the unique situation of each project, but overuse without alteration becomes report padding. Try to make the boilerplate sensitive to any unique situations in an area.

FROM DRAFT TO FINAL REPORT

If the CRM project is small, the only readers may be the contracting agency and the SHPO's review and compliance department. Longer reports, usually from testing and mitigation projects, get read by more people. Many federal agencies tend to have deadlines for various draft versions of the report, so when it comes to differences of opinion about the content and format of a report, most elements are negotiable. If you've maintained good relationships with the contracting officer, agency, and SHPO, minor problems can quickly be dealt with. More difficult matters, such as whether your project actually met the scope or your proposal, may not be easily handled, but if you've kept the various parties informed, even they can be overcome.

When it comes to reports, do your best to meet the needs of all parties, particularly if you hope to have other contracts with them in the future. Certainly, someone does read all your reports, which may include many of your peers and competitors. Make suggested changes where they are reasonable, but be sure the contracting agency knows why you didn't make other changes. In the highly stressful world of CRM, you'll live longer if you don't get bent out about every little thing!

GETTING YOUR CRM REPORT NOTICED

Getting your report noticed beyond an agency or region is often difficult. However, you should make an effort to be certain some notice of your report is available beyond just a line on your résumé or vita. Some state archaeological society newsletters or journals contain sections set aside specifically to list recent CRM reports and abstracts. In the United States, the Reports module of the National Park Service's National Archeological Database

> is an expanded bibliographic inventory of approximately 240,000 reports on archeological investigation and planning, mostly of limited circulation. This 'gray literature' represents a large portion of the primary information available on archeological sites in the U.S. NADB-Reports can be searched by state, county, worktype, cultural affiliation, keyword, material, year of publication, title, and author. (National Park Service 2000)

The database is profoundly useful and an excellent way of being sure people know about CRM projects in each state. Reports from federal agencies increasingly are being made available on line in full text using portable document files (.pdf).

JOURNAL ARTICLES AND BOOK CHAPTERS

Professional journal articles and book chapters are the heart and soul of the theoretical side of both CRM and academic archaeology. Producing them is more difficult than CRM reports because they are less "formulaic," though the deadlines usually are more flexible and there may be fewer peer reviewers.

JOURNAL ARTICLES

Journals are widely variable in topic and scope within archaeology, so your initial task is finding a journal appropriate for your manuscript. If you are near a university campus with a good library, you'll find it worth your time to visit regularly to go through the journals to which the library subscribes, or you can look for the journal on the web. (See the appendix for a listing of the URLs for some archaeology journals with websites.)

STATE JOURNALS AND NEWSLETTERS

Certainly, if your manuscript is mostly a descriptive report on an archaeological site or artifact with limited interest outside the area, the best fit may be in one of the many good local or state archaeological society journals. If you've got a short, localized contribution, perhaps the newsletter of the society would be even better.

State and local journals or newsletters contain a lot of terrific archaeology, often of more use to scholars than articles in major journals. They also usually have a need for material, and time from submission to publication is often substantially less than that for major journals. One reason is that they are rarely peer reviewed.

REGIONAL JOURNALS

Regional journals cover a wide range of material, from site reports to methodological to theoretical as they relate specifically to an area or region. For archaeology in the United States, these regions are often roughly congruent with culture areas. In existence since the 1950s, *Plains Anthropologist,* for example, publishes archaeology and some Plains ethnography. Articles in regional journals tend to be peer reviewed; most usually deal with subjects that have utility and implications for the broader region rather than more limited locales. Regional journals work well ahead of deadlines, so you can probably plan on a minimum of six to eight months before your article comes out.

TOPICAL JOURNALS

Topical journals tend to consider issues surrounding a subject matter defined by a methodological or theoretical concern that crosscuts regional or national boundaries. This might be something like field methods, as is the case in the *Journal of Field Archaeology,* or issues surrounding archaeological and heritage management in the public sphere, as are considered in *Public Archaeology.*

If you have a manuscript that is topical, be sure that the subject matter fits the types of materials covered by the journal. If in doubt, you might send an inquiry to the editor asking whether he or she will look at the manuscript or an abstract before sending it out for peer review.

"BIG-TIME" JOURNALS

Big-time journals are those that tend to be recognized by most archaeologists as the major and prestigious journals in the field. Most are published by professional organizations. For example, most archaeologists in the Americas and the rest of the world recognize *American Antiquity* and *Latin American Antiquity*, published by the Society for American Archaeology, as key journals. On a world basis, most regard *Antiquity* as important. Many also acknowledge general anthropology journals such as *American Anthropologist* or *Current Anthropology* as publishers of important archaeological articles, although they publish articles in all subfields of anthropology.

As you might imagine, these journals are the most difficult ones in which to publish, not entirely because they always contain the best pieces but because of the competition. Quality is generally better than many journals; the number of submissions is high. Although some attention is given to fair coverage of archaeological time periods or regions, articles with theoretical, methodological, and topical content useful to a wider audience tend to be published before others. In truth, unless your article has broad implications for the field, you may find a wider readership for it in a topical or regional journal. However, if you are an academic, worried about earning promotion and tenure, there is enough elitism in most institutions to warrant the effort of submitting articles to the more prestigious journals. Be prepared for turnaround time from first submission to publication of a year or more.

EDITED VOLUMES AND BOOK CHAPTERS

Edited volumes contain a series of papers or chapters compiled around a certain theme. Topics are as variable as all the possible ideas or themes in archaeology. Edited volumes are sometimes the spawn of a conference session from which all or the best papers are drawn; sometimes extra, solicited papers get added to the mix.

Whatever the origin, writing book chapters is much like writing journal articles. Book editors have a difficult job, especially when it comes to writing style. Edited volumes, just like journals, are notoriously uneven in the content of articles and writing. Good editors generally try to make your piece fit the whole. If an editor suggests changes in your writing in order to bring your chapter into the volume's writing style, just do it. The only time you should fight this is when the suggested change significantly alters your meaning.

Book chapters are carefully reviewed by the volume editor(s). In addition, sometimes the publisher will send the whole volume out for review to anonymous reviewers.

NOTES, REPORTS, AND NEWSLETTERS

Most organizations have some kind of newsletter for keeping members informed. These contain everything from editorials, letters to the editor, committee reports, obituaries, job ads, conference notices, cooperation columns, and shorter articles of a narrow focus. Some journals publish notes or reports, which tend to be very focused, and short articles, usually fewer than five published pages, describing a new discovery or discussing a new methodological or interpretive technique. Turnaround time on these is usually more rapid than for articles, and some journals do not submit them to extensive peer review, if they are reviewed outside the editorial staff at all. For younger scholars, submitting pieces as notes or reports may be less stressful than trying to publish articles in the prestigious journals right away.

BOOK REVIEWS

Most journals also publish book reviews. Reviews help readers allocate their time (and money) by giving clues as to what may or may not be a useful volume. For younger scholars, being contacted to write a review is relatively rare, so don't wait for it to happen. Some journals ask potential reviewers to identify themselves. Another approach is a bit more aggressive, but if you know of a book that has just been published, you might contact the review editor and ask to do the review.

Book reviews may be a good place for younger scholars to start publishing. However, book reviews are not as easy to write as some might think because of limited space. Consider yourself fortunate if you are allowed more than two hundred to four hundred words.

As a reviewer, you generally get to keep the book after the review. If you agree to do a review, be certain to do it! When I served as book review editor for *Plains Anthropologist,* about a quarter of the books I sent out never got reviewed, even after several reminders. Here are some other matters to consider:

- Don't agree to do a review unless you can be completely fair.
- Do the review by the deadline, or make arrangements for returning the book or for an extension.
- Stay close to the word limit.
- Don't focus on petty issues of production unless they truly detract from the book's content.
- Pay special attention to the arguments made by the book. Do they make sense?
- Don't simply repeat the dust jacket blurbs that promote the book. Analyze critically.
- Remember that just about every book has both good and bad points.
- Remember that what goes around, comes around. The author whose book you review today may review yours tomorrow.

One variation is the review essay, in which a reviewer examines, compares, and contrasts a number of books centering on a theme, published at about the same time. These are sometimes more difficult to write but do provide for interesting comparisons and are almost articles in themselves. They allow a reviewer to include his or her own analytical constructs in addition to reviewing the books. In recent years, more journals are including reviews of videos, computer programs, museum exhibits, and multimedia. If you are asked or request to do such a review, remember that these media are different from books and may require different expertise.

BOOKS AND MONOGRAPHS

Monographs tend to be specialized treatises on very narrow subjects, such as a lengthy discussion of a particular class of objects or an extended version of a site report. Books tend to be more general in coverage, perhaps an analysis of a particular theoretical approach or theme, using examples from several archaeological sites or regions.

A monograph often represents the culmination of a relatively narrow analytical project resulting from something such as a grant or contract, while a book may begin out of your interest in a particular research topic, more comprehensive and synthetic than most monographs tend to be. Monographs also tend to be published by more specialized presses, such as in a museum or university press series. Most monographs also tend to have a relatively smaller number of pages than books. The press run (the number of copies printed) also tends to be small, usually a few hundred. If you intend to publish a monograph, you'll probably need to have the full manuscript completed before you contact anyone about publishing the work. University presses and museums are likely monograph publishers, because they are not in business to make a profit. Some commercial scientific publishers also will have monograph series.

Books tend to be longer and have larger print runs, but this depends mostly on the publisher and the topic of the volume. Books often begin life as a prospectus rather than a finished manuscript. A *prospectus* is essentially a proposal to a publisher to produce a manuscript on a particular topic. The format of a prospectus is fairly standard across the industry, but with enough variation that you may wish to write a publisher for its requirements. Most ask for these items:

- A description of the volume
- An assessment of the intended audience
- An assessment of the "competition"—that is, other books similar to the one you are proposing
- A table of contents
- A completion schedule

Some publishers also ask for a writing sample, especially if the book is to be single authored. They may request names of possible reviewers, too.

The press will usually send the prospectus to reviewers to ask their opinion, and depending on what they write, the press may offer a contract. The process may take some time, so be prepared for a wait of several months depending on the reviewers and the publisher's decision-making process.

Pick your possible publisher wisely. Find out which publishers are publishing in your area or topic. This may be as easy as looking on your bookshelf. Looking online or at a few catalogs from a publisher may give you more information, or you might also ask a well-published colleague. You should also consider the amount of advertising a publisher does to market books.

If you've done much publishing, you've probably already made lots of mistakes. For example, when it came to publishing my dissertation a quarter-century ago, I accepted the first offer that came along to publish it, in a solid but not well-recognized or well-marketed state series. After I heard that the monograph was being used in several classes and it had gotten some good reviews, I realized that I probably could have gotten it published in the "hot" New Archaeology press of that era. That might have done more for the early years of my career. Most recently, a colleague and I did a trade book (a book for general audiences). The book is beautiful, with lots of color illustrations, and inexpensive. We accepted a generous one-time payment up front. However, after the U.S. publisher let it go out of print after selling ten thousand copies, another U.S. publisher picked it up, marketed it better, and in just over six months sold thousands more. We've also learned that our book was translated into other languages. We would have done much better if we had bargained a bit on contractual matters. Most academics are so eager to see their names in print anywhere that they often don't even consider the question of royalties, republication rights, and the like.

Monographs usually don't pay and are often financial losers for the publishers. Books and monographs published by university presses and commercial scholarly presses will often pay royalties, but the chances of making much money are slight. The structure is widely variable, usually a percentage of sales, sometimes incrementally increased as sales move up. Trade books are a different ball game altogether, with substantially higher sales numbers and more generous royalties.

If a publisher offers you a contract, do your best to honor its terms. If you suspect that there will be problems, make a point of keeping in regular contact with your publisher.

THE MADDENING TRIVIA: PROOF PAGES AND INDEXES

As you work through the book publication process, you'll face two issues that can make you crazy: proofs and indexes.

The proofs are the final step of your work as an author. They are actual mock-ups of the pages of your book or article. The publisher sends them to you for a final look before the manuscript gets printed.

Read proofs carefully! They are ultimately your responsibility. More embarrassing screw-ups happen here than anywhere else in the publishing process. Sometimes you do a diligent job proofreading the text, but forget the big stuff, such as the cover. In my own case, my middle initial (*J*) has been *A* once (my own fault) and *W* (my coeditor's fault) on covers.

There are lots of tried and true techniques for reading proofs. Some suggest reading the text backward; other say that they need to be read aloud to another person who follows with the last submitted version before proofs. Why these techniques? You are too close to the material and know what it's supposed to say. If you silently read the proofs, you tend to fill in with what is correct instead of recognizing errors.

Finally, by the time you are at the proof stage, the only changes you can make are minor. Most publishers allow minor changes of a word or two, but anything that changes pagination, especially for journals, may not be allowed or may be allowed but with a charge. Most publishers only give a few days for reading proofs.

Most book contracts require you as author or editor to provide an index of the volume based on the page proofs. Resist the temptation to rely solely on electronic indexing using your word processor files. They will index proper nouns but not necessarily choose the words you want or order them as you wish. Go through a manuscript and enter the terms and subterms alphabetically on your word processor, listing the page numbers as you go. If you are working with several authors and time allows, you can also ask them to highlight the terms in the proofs that they find to be important.

Some publishers will provide indexes done by professional indexers, but because they don't know what's important in your field, they may not do as good a job as you. Publishers will usually charge you for a professionally prepared index. Remember how often you use indexes, and you'll know how important the task is.

PUBLISHING AND CAREER DEVELOPMENT

If you are a young or soon-to-be professional archaeologist, you'll get lots of advice from people on how to develop your publishing career: Only books really count; publish only journal articles; publish both, but only with the best publishers or journals; avoid popular media; don't do edited volumes; and so on. The truth is that in many cases, opportunity is what guides you, not your own plan. Let's say you've just finished a dissertation, just read by a big name in the field who invites you to submit a manuscript for a chapter in a book she's editing. Do you turn her down because your mentor told you to do only books? Frankly, to do so would be nuts! Opportunity doesn't knock all that often, so sometimes you have to allow for the serendipitous.

One good way is to devise a "lifetime" research plan. Look realistically at your career goals and your interests, then figure out how to reach them. Do you hope to find an academic job at a top-flight university by the time you are thirty-five? Do you like CRM enough to stay in it your whole career as the owner of your own firm? Your publications need to be geared to allow you to accomplish your research needs and your career ambitions, but it won't happen overnight. Plan a realistic and relatively loose schedule, allowing for some changes in goals as your interests change and opportunities shift, but still fulfill your ethical obligation to be accountable to the public.

If you are disciplined, you can really do a lot of writing. If you write only five hundred finished words (about two double-spaced pages) daily, that's seven hundred manuscript pages a year, the equivalent of two to three books or twenty articles every year! That will make you one of the most published people in archaeology. Be even half that productive, and there will be time to meet most needs for individual research plans, obligations to the public, and career ambitions, as well as to have a little fun! To make this happen, you need to learn to do the following:

1. Do research that will be usable for several works. You may need to finish a CRM report right now, but the research about the culture history of the river drainage in which you are working can be used for your future book on the archaeology of your state.
2. Consider multiple outlets for the same piece of work. The people who won't read that methodological article on Clovis point manufacture in *American Antiquity* might be interested in that unique point from central South Dakota you discuss in *South Dakota Archaeology.*
3. Mix the level of publication types. A good mix of professional and popular articles and varying lengths of publications make you well rounded and someone meeting both professional and public obligations.
4. Start small and work up. You don't need to hit the big-time journals right away. Graduate students publishing in the state journal or newsletter will be well ahead of most of their cohort. As a

young professional, you can work toward publishing in journals at the national level as well as writing books.

5. Don't be afraid to collaborate. As an archaeologist, you often work as a member of a team, so why not publish as a team member? Pick reliable collaborators.

Lots of people can help you with your career—mentors, colleagues, friends, and spouses—so don't be afraid to ask them what they think or to work with you on some project. Another who will sometimes seem like an enemy, but who is really one of your best friends in the whole process, is the editor.

EDITING AND THE PUBLICATION PROCESS

There always seems to be a level of tension between writers and editors, and it's probably good that there is. In college and graduate school, you wrote papers at deadlines, allowing little time for feedback. Most of us didn't face an editor until we submitted a manuscript for publication and didn't quite know how to react to real criticism.

In fact, many of us see criticism of our work as bad, not something that can help us improve. Few actually *like* to see their work criticized. At the same time, constructive criticism is extremely useful, especially for writing. As you write, you are so close to the process and product that you have difficulty seeing flaws of structure, poor word choice, and even typographical errors. As an exercise, find an old paper you've written for a class, an old CRM report, or something else you've written that you were pleased with at the time. Read it. After you are finished, try to honestly assess your feelings about it. Unless you have extraordinary writing skill (or an extremely strong ego!), you'll probably not like what you read. Time away from the piece has given you distance and a better perspective.

SELF-EDITING

As I age, I find that I'm my own worst editor. That has its strengths but sometimes can be debilitating. A major strength is that I don't send any of my writing out of my office until I've rewritten it several times. I've revised the manuscript for this book four or five times before I let my series coeditor, Bill Green, even glance at it. Using Word, I'll Flesch-

Kincaid Index (a readability index with my word processor) a few paragraphs at random to see whether I'm hitting about the right audience
level (grade level 8.5 for this paragraph, by the way). I've learned to use
my word processor's grammar checker, and you should, too. I'll throw
out entire sections because they just plain suck (but keep them in a dis-
card file in case I can use a revised version of what I throw away). Most
of the time, I feel relatively confident and just make minor changes,
such as moving a paragraph around, changing words here and there, and
sometimes expanding an idea.

For self-editing, at least give yourself a few days before you reread
something editorially. Your best editing happens after some time has
elapsed. Another good piece of advice is to read aloud what you've
written. If it sounds stilted or if sentence structure sounds convoluted, it probably is. Read *exactly* what is written on the page or
screen because your mind sometimes rewrites what you see on paper.
Editing on-screen is difficult. To save paper, do an editorial read on
screen, but eventually print a rough copy and edit that. You'll often
find more problems.

COLLEAGUES AND FRIENDS AS EDITORS

Once you've done what you can to clean up your work, you need
to move on to the hard part: letting someone else read what you've
written. Most people find this hard to do. Letting someone else read
what you've done brings a fear of criticism, but it's really more than
that. Writing is a display of your logical and reasoning skills, your
scholarly abilities, and, at some level, your "soul." Who wouldn't be
afraid?

Get over the fear by having classmates, friends, or close colleagues
read your work before putting it into the peer review system. Be
aware that people close to you can be harsh critics, so you might prepare yourself for that. In my Ph.D. grad school classes, even though
all of us in seminars were pretty good friends, we used to delight in
criticizing each other's work. We joked about razor-sharp Marshall-
town trowels flashing in the light like sacrificial knives ready to rip
the heart out of each other's papers over typos and poor word choices.
If you understand that this is not meant to be hurtful, you can deal
with it pretty easily and get used to criticism meant as it should be:
a way to improve your thinking and writing. If you're uncomfortable
with criticism, start with friends because the peer review system *can*

be worse.

PEER REVIEW

Peer review—examination of your work by colleagues who know something about your subject area—can be one of the most traumatic parts of professional writing, even for seasoned professionals with lots of publications. Most professional journals and most reputable academic publishers send your manuscript out to a "jury" of your peers. In the CRM world, an agency might send your report out to several colleagues from the area to see whether your colleagues think you did the project and report at professional standards.

The trauma of peer review is exacerbated by the fact that peer review is often anonymous; that is, the reviewers don't get identified unless they choose to tell you who they are. In theory, the idea of anonymity is important because it allows reviewers to really write what they think about a manuscript, without fear of retribution from the author.

If all parties act professionally, anonymous peer review serves an important purpose by assuring that what gets published is of high quality. There is more to peer review than publish/don't publish recommendations. Most journals or publishers have a set series of questions, which, if answered faithfully by a reviewer, can help an author solve problems of logic, writing, and scholarship, as well as to suggest additional questions or interpretations. The problems for authors arise when reviewers don't do a good job or allow their personal biases to overshadow their professional responsibility to the author.

Some people take delight in skewering colleagues over their work, a tendency anonymous peer review makes easy. I make a point of signing all my reviews of the work of others, especially when the author is someone who is not my favorite person. I do this because I believe that I need to be responsible for my opinions. Manuscripts that don't have some redeeming quality are rare. If you can't say something nice, at least offer some suggestions on how to improve the work.

Sometimes there are also legitimate differences of opinion, and sometimes the result can be almost amusing, even if frustrating, when, for example, two reviewers like or dislike exactly the opposite papers in an edited volume or recommend changes to a manuscript that would do exactly the opposite of what the other suggests. Tom

Biolsi and I coedited a series of conference papers, ultimately published in 1997 by the University of Arizona Press (UAP) as *Indians and Anthropologists: Vine Deloria, Jr. and the Critique of Anthropology.* We sent the manuscript to another press first, which used two peer reviewers. Both reviews came back negative, each really disliking *exactly* the opposite group of papers. None of them suggested any changes except dumping the papers they didn't like. On that basis, the press rejected the book. We then sent the manuscript to UAP along with the reviews from the other press. With the earlier reviews in hand, UAP sent the collection out to two more reviewers, and virtually the same thing happened, but with this, UAP realized that the reason was not that the papers were bad but that the subject was controversial. They have reprinted the book after the first run sold out. For us, the process was traumatic and frustrating, but not without humor.

FINAL STEPS IN THE PROCESS

The last editorial barriers involve the editor, copyeditor, publisher, or contracting agency. An editor takes peer review comments, reads the work, and then may demand, ask for, or negotiate any substantive changes. After you've agreed on changes and resubmitted the manuscript, a copyeditor usually goes over it in detail looking for contradictions, missing elements, and spelling, typographical, grammatical, or stylistic errors. The copyeditor will be certain that your manuscript meets their style guide, to which you already should have paid attention. Sometimes, especially if a manuscript has few changes to make, both the editor and copyeditor do their work before asking you to resubmit a clean version. After making these changes and resubmitting, your work is nearly done. You may get page proofs to examine one last time for errors or to incorporate very small additional changes you'd like to make. Books may involve the added step of indexing.

These stages may seem straightforward, but there can be problems. The greatest danger comes when you get reviewer and editorial comments back and simply can't face them. You've already spent so much time on a manuscript and are so close to it that making changes is just about the last thing you want to do. If you don't get to the changes quickly, you might not get to them at all. Knowing this, many editors give you time limits at various stages of the process. I rather like the maxim a colleague uses to motivate himself: "If I don't get on top of it, it gets on top of me." Get the work done as soon as possible.

The role of the editor in the publishing process is crucial. His job is to present a work to a reader that is clear, consistent, and clean. You will rarely run into an editor who wants to change your work dramatically, and good editors want to keep your style as much as possible. When Mitch Allen at AltaMira Press worked with Bill Green and me on the Archaeologist's Toolkit series, we agreed beforehand that we needed to maintain as much as possible a general style and tone in the books. They were not to be academic treatises but more like primers. We wanted them to be as lively as possible. We understood that with nearly a dozen authors and coauthors, we absolutely would not be able to control this, and we knew we would get a range of writing styles. We agreed on certain conventions of presentation such as bulleted lists, cross-references, and boxes.

The editor's job largely deals with content and style, while the copyeditor's is in the details. Copyeditors are the real workhorses of the publishing world. Pay attention: They usually know more about grammar and style than you do! Still, they can make errors because they are usually not experts in the content of a field—but I've not met a copyeditor yet who has not improved my work.

Having worked as a university press director, an editor, and an author, I'd say that the author causes more problems than editors ever do. Usually troubles stem from an author's attitude. Many authors, especially those less seasoned but sometimes even experienced writers, think that everything they write is wonderful. Younger writers usually just have worked so hard on something that they can't imagine it could be improved by editing. To reiterate: I've never read a manuscript that could not be improved by a good editor. Whatever the case, I urge authors to be humble enough to be flexible. Work with your editors, not against them!

BEING AN EDITOR

Sometimes you may end up on the other side, editing a manuscript. Doing CRM reports today is often a team project, with specialists in everything from ethnobotany to remote sensing. For a final report, you may have to serve as an editor for the other people's sections. You may also find yourself being an editor of a set of chapters sent to a publisher. You may be selected as a journal editor. As an editor, you also need to be humble enough to be flexible. Certainly, you do have power. Don't abuse it; to do so is unethical and will not serve archaeology well.

You have a right to respect and an obligation to be certain that the best possible work goes into the journal or volume. You will face the arrogant or stubborn author. I once had an excellent paper submitted to me as editor of *Plains Anthropologist*, but it needed a couple of important changes. I would have been embarrassed if the paper had appeared without them. The author was adamant about not making the changes, so I agreed to publish the paper as it was, but only if I could add a statement at the bottom of the first page that certain changes had been recommend but not made by the author. The author made the changes before it went to print.

You'll face the other problems of materials getting back to you on time or not getting back at all. The peer review process is the worst of it. Establish a time frame and stick to it. If a reviewer doesn't respond, find another quickly.

Despite the problems, journal and volume editors do an important job in archaeology by evaluating and distributing important works. Editing reinforces the importance of collaboration and, believe it or not, builds respect for colleagues. Editing brings other rewards as well. The contacts they allow can be important for building your career. Caring, competent, and patient editors with a solid sense of humor make far more friends than enemies. Editing is a tough job, but something every archaeologist needs to try, if only once.

10

BRINGING THE PAST TO LIFE AND PRESENTING IT WITH STYLE

For all the fine writing we may do as professional archaeologists, the public mostly finds our writing boring, or at least overly complex. For people who have never seen or tried flint knapping, no written explanation is sufficient to help them understand the process, even if an archaeologist is masterful at creating images from words. The minute they see and try real flint knapping, the better they understand both the process and our explanations of it. The same applies to our discussions of how people in the past lived. Mostly our work describes the norms of life in the past; individuals and their feelings are usually absent from what we present. Sometimes we forget that objects aren't people, a major complaint about archaeology from members of descendent communities.

We know why we do this: Our data are limited, and we feel that they don't justify saying more. Should we even try to get past the limits? As scientists, we don't like to speculate too much. After all, if we do, we'll probably face the criticism and the disdain of our peers. That's what makes many of us shy away from popularizing archaeology. Archaeologists seem to have a love–hate relationship with our popularizers. As in other sciences, some of us have smeared colleagues who popularize science (e.g., Carl Sagan). Are we jealous of their skill, celebrity, or earnings? At the same time, most of us also know what a useful service they perform for a public that believes most of us "suck the life" out of what can be really interesting stuff. I was recently shocked when three of my colleagues who teach introductory prehistory proclaimed how boring the class was.

If the professor thinks the class is boring, pity the poor students! Maybe our critics are right: We must find solutions to the deadening effect we have on archaeology. Fortunately, some of our colleagues have found ways to put life back into the dusty old bones. The first step is to understand that hands-on learning works well.

HANDS-ON LEARNING PROMOTES UNDERSTANDING

The old saw that seeing is believing contains a major truth. I've tried and tried to explain a spear thrower to students. There is never any real understanding until I bring atlatls and darts for the students to use. After the initial fear of making fools of themselves dissipates, their eyes light up when they start to get the hang of the instrument and see the increased range and impact of a spear. This is the same reason, of course, that we organize field schools. All the book descriptions and drawings of stratigraphy, for example, mean nothing compared to having to read soil layers in a cut bank. If there is a way to use hands-on techniques in any public venue, do it!

Hands-on experience may be as simple as passing around a few artifacts or reproductions when you give that service organization lunch talk discussed in chapter 8 or having a small display of objects people can touch or handle before or after your talk. If there is a way for people to do or handle things safely, work this in. This is no big secret—learning sometimes comes better with doing than with reading or listening.

ACTION IS BETTER THAN DESCRIPTION

Dig magazine does a masterful job at drawing the reader into thinking about life in the past, not archaeology. For example, the short news piece on a child's footprints found in Chauvet Cave in France that I discussed in chapter 4 about writing styles is a fine example of much of the magazine's writing. Let's look at the statement again:

> About 20,000–30,000 years ago, an 8- to 10-year-old boy skidded barefoot through a muddy cave in what is now southern France. Think that kid would get a kick out of knowing that his tootsie marks would become the oldest footprints ever found in Europe?

The first sentence sets the action, and the second draws the reader directly into the thoughts of that child from millennia ago. Of course, we don't write this way for our colleagues or advanced students, but perhaps we ought to do more of it for our entry-level students and the general public.

Our public talks should try to pull the listeners into the action. Often this might be no more difficult than the sentence from *Dig*: "Think that kid would . . . ?" You might be able to enliven archaeology by making connections directly to the current lives or memories of listeners and readers. You can draw links to objects they are familiar with in their daily lives, or even do something as simple as ask them what they are reminded of when they see an artifact. This might be introduced by a question such as "Did you ever wonder . . . ?" This approach involves the audience directly in the substance of your presentation, with choices to make about what you say. Action makes archaeology interactive; the reader or listener becomes a partner in the product (this is a crucial concept for new media, as will be discussed in chapter 12).

GAMES AND TOYS

The popularity of hands-on activities makes games and toys almost ideal media for archaeology, but we rarely think of them as ways to bring life to the past. Some involve simulated excavation. One good example is Running Press's 1994 *Lost Civilizations Explorer's Kit* in which you use a Popsicle stick "trowel" to excavate a miniature Mayan ruin from Tikal. The accompanying booklet tells how real excavations get done and provides other activities such as making a *Patolli* board game played by the Aztec and Maya. Another activity is writing in Mayan hieroglyphs. Similarly, *Our Amazing Ancestors Science Kit,* published by Educational Designs, Inc. (1997), deals with a much earlier period. Twenty-four activities range from putting Amazing Ancestor stamps on a six-foot-long time chart to making and painting small plaster casts of fossil skulls and cave painting. There is also instruction on how to make and play "Out of Africa," a board game about (pre)human migration.

Older children and some adults enjoy role-playing games. One that's fun is *Tribes: It's 50,000 B.C.—Where Are Your Children?* published by Steve Jackson Games (1998) and written by science fiction writer David Brin and Steve Jackson. Each player represents a tribesperson. The object of the game is biological success—that is, to reproduce and have many children reach adulthood. The game's rules teach many concepts of early cultural evolution.

Computer games are sometimes variations of role-playing games. Microsoft's *Age of Empire* series is a terrific strategy game with several modules in which players build and maintain empires. For all its silliness about Atlantis, the game segments of GTE Entertainment's *Timelapse* are pretty good graphically and factually for Egypt, the Maya, the Anasazi, and Easter Island. McGraw-Hill Home Interactive's *Pyramid: Challenge of the Pharoah's Dream* is funny and surprisingly accurate regarding Egyptian culture, tools, pyramid building, and daily life along the Nile. Players use math, science, and logic to solve problems. The Lara Croft action–adventure series is more stereotypical than useful, but the games are fun.

With all games and toys, most archaeologists are likely to worry about accuracy. If so, we might consider suggesting games or serving as technical advisers for them. Creating a few may help you develop interesting activities for the public, and you may even find a market for them.

ARCHAEOLOGICAL FICTION

Some archaeologists and other authors have taken the approach that fiction can be used to teach as well as entertain. After all, we rarely get glimpses of individuals from the past and often wonder what they must have been like. We might even fantasize about having a time machine to allow more intimate glimpses into the past and how people acted, thought, and felt. We know they have a story. Archaeologist John Whittaker (1992:56–58), for example, discusses the archaeology of the Sinagua, a prehistoric complex of the American Southwest that may be related to the Anasazi. He writes, "Few of us would bother with archaeology if we weren't emotionally involved with the past. We don't dig for dry bones and dusty potsherds, but for people. . . . I care about them and want to tell their story." Most of us agree, but while we crave that knowledge, we understand there is no real way to know the past. Fortunately, several writers are willing to try to help us understand what life may have been like. They write short stories and novels, and by doing so, they help us make connections between the humanity of past lives and our own.

Writing fiction is absorbing, exhilarating, and mostly humbling. I can't say much about the process, except that I've published one short story about archaeology (Zimmerman 1986) and have several failed starts of a novel. Novels require a delicate balance between character and plot, connected by vast amounts of hard work and creativity. Although there are numerous bad novels about archaeology, there are also many good ones (see sidebar 10.1). Authors of the good ones do solid research before each book, and while scholars might nay-say some elements, most of each story rings true.

Plenty of books are available on how to write fiction. If you want to try it, read a few books and jump in. I'm glad that some authors are willing to give archaeological fiction a shot. We need them.

10.1. RECOMMENDED ARCHAEOLOGICAL NOVELS

- W. Michael and Kathleen O'Neal Gear
  Two CRM archaeologists have turned their imagination to the North American past in their extremely popular First North Americans series (titles contain *People of . . .*) and the Anasazi Mysteries series, both published by Tom Doherty Associates.
- William Sarabande
  The First Americans (Bantam Books) series details lives of some of America's first inhabitants.
- Kathleen King
  Cricket Sings: A Novel of Pre-Columbian Cahokia (Ohio University Press, 1983).
- Jean Auel
  Clan of the Cave Bear, the first and best of her The Earth's Children series (Crown, 1980).
- Piers Anthony
  Tatham Mound. Fantasy author turns his attention to the impact of the DeSoto expedition on Florida's Native populations (Morrow, 1991).
- Sharman Apt Russell
  Essayist turned some of her research for the nonfiction *When the Land Was Young: Reflections on American Archaeology* (Addison-Wesley, 1996) into *The Last Matriarch* (New Mexico, 2000), a novel of the American Southwest eleven thousand years ago.

CARTOONS

Most archaeologists probably don't consider cartoons to be a medium for communicating with the public, but cartoons can be an effective way of communicating a point. Most of us have pinned a Gary Larson cartoon from *The Far Side* on our bulletin board at one time or another. Bill Tidy's cartoons for *Archaeology* magazine or Robert Humphrey's in *AnthroNotes* bring a chuckle. Tidy has teamed with archaeologist Paul Bahn for a longer, raunchy, and hysterically funny treatment of human history in *Disgraceful Archaeology* (Bahn and Tidy 1999). Segments of Larry Gonick's (1990) *The Cartoon History of the Universe* provide a fair summary of human cultural evolution in comic form. The best and most hilariously to the point in terms of demonstrating archaeological thinking is David Macaulay's (1979) *Motel of the Mysteries* with an excavation of the Toot-N-Come-On Motel in the year 4022.

Cartoons allow an easy connection between the past and contemporary life through the use of anachronisms and humor. They make us think in slightly different ways, usually with a good laugh. To do cartooning requires relatively modest artistic talent and an ability to quickly find a core message. Some archaeologists can do this well as part of their "doodling." If it comes easily, you might consider adding cartoons to your repertoire of ways to present the past.

MOVIES AND VIDEOS:
LIVE ACTION VERSUS DOCUMENTARY

Just as most archaeologists don't consider writing fiction, most also don't consider making movies. Certainly, most of us understand the impact of the movies on our profession. The astounding success of *Raiders of the Lost Ark* and its sequels showed the influence of films in bringing archaeology to public attention. Generations of movie-goers have seen archaeologists as eccentric pith- or fedora-helmeted treasure hunters. Portrayals of archaeologists differ little from the opening scenes of Boris Karloff's 1933 *The Mummy* through today's *Tomb Raider* video game, spin-off movie, and Lara Croft action figures. (At least more women archaeologists are being portrayed.)

We might not always like the way our profession or our methods get portrayed in theatrical films, but the only way to fight this is to work with the motion picture industry—a fight we won't win because stereotypes sell. On the other hand, by turning the subject of our work into screenplay, we have a better chance. Even though it was a box office flop, consider *Rapa Nui,* the movie about Easter Island. It did a respectable job of showing a possible way of building and transporting the *moai,* the huge stone heads raised by the people of the island, and it put life into oral tradition, environmental reconstructions, and a wide range of good archaeological issues. Archaeologists can serve as technical consultants on such movies. Perhaps more of us should also suggest topics to the movie industry, and a few of us might even try writing a screenplay. For those interested in doing screenplays, books and even software on how to do them can easily be found by doing a web search using the terms *writing* and *screenplay* together.

Archaeologists should consider making documentaries about our work. Easter Island provides another good example of how this can be done. The 1998 Nova documentary *The Secrets of Easter Island* shows the other side of the *Rapa Nui* coin. The video focuses on the work of Jo Anne Van Tilburg and others, often using experimental archaeology. The spin-off website for the program at www.pbs.org/wgbh/nova/easter/ provides a wealth of print and interactive material, including a small video game simulating life on the island, use of natural resources, and building moai. With the American public getting most of its information about archaeology from television, and with cable channels such as Discovery Channel, the Learning Channel, and the History Channel each needing well over one hundred hours of programming a week, there is a definite market for archaeology documentaries.

The problem, as with writing novels or screenplays, is that few of us have any training in preparing documentaries. Filmmaking is a full-time occupation requiring years of training. At the same time, most of us can be extremely useful in providing story ideas to documentary producers or acting as technical consultants (see chapter 11). And now, with affordable digital video cameras and quality video-editing software, creating your own documentary is not difficult. You won't likely be able to prepare a broadcast-quality documentary, but you might be able to prepare good, compelling work for your classes, a museum, or some other local venue.

Seek out quality sources for help. A terrific one is Barry Hampe's *Making Documentary Films and Reality Videos: A Practical Guide to Planning, Filming, and Editing Documentaries of Real Events* (published by Owlet, 1997). Hampe discusses preproduction (developing ideas, writing at various stages, scheduling, etc.), production (recording picture and sound, directing, interviewing, etc.), and postproduction (preparation, editing, and the wrap) phases of filmmaking. He writes about selecting equipment, hiring necessary crew, directing actors and nonactors, and conducting on-camera interviews. Although the process might seem daunting, Hampe shows how to plan, recognize, and record visual evidence and how to organize it into a visual argument. I'll admit that I've not yet tried anything lengthy, but I have worked on a couple of commercials for a powwow, and I'd like to do more.

Working as a consultant or interviewee on a video can be a bit intimidating. I've now consulted on several programs, and I've been on camera several times. The most difficult work was for the BBC Horizon program *Bones of Contention*. The taping had a separate audio track, a video track, the traditional movie clapboard, and just about everything else needed for a movie. A thoroughly professional crew and director can often help you along, and after a couple of takes, you don't feel so strange, though I'd not like to do it as a regular part of my job.

The beauty of video is that you can reach a large audience and not have to be there. Seeing a video can bring life to the past, but it still can't substitute for being a part of the past or, more appropriately, interacting with the past. There is no substitute for a real hands-on activity like what one can get in a school classroom, a museum, or "archaeology days" activities.

PUBLIC ARCHAEOLOGY

For eight years, the University of South Dakota (USD) Archaeology Laboratory worked with the Vermillion, South Dakota, Middle School on a project we called "Archaeology Days" (Zimmerman et al. 1994) Collaborating with the sixth-grade teachers, we literally took over the curriculum for about two weeks. Teachers primed the kids with readings in their literature books, some videos, and a large lunchroom display about archaeology, but the core was hands-on activities. One full day was devoted to ancient technologies and another to fieldwork in the plow zone of a heavily disturbed site. The project had an impact. The kids saw the connections between their areas of learning. The teachers were full of stories about changed interests and behaviors.

The USD project is but one example of many. Several excellent books provide educational contexts and ideas for doing similar projects. *The Archaeology Education Handbook: Sharing the Past with Kids* (Smardz and Smith 2000) is a guidebook aimed at educating children in archaeology. *Presenting Archaeology to the Public: Digging for Truths* (Jameson 1997) provides case studies of ways to translate archaeological information for broader public audiences. The SAA provides a wide range of public education materials on its website at www.saa.org/education/edumat.html. Of special note is the *Archaeology and Public Education Newsletter* available on the web at www.saa.org/PubEdu/a&pe. The SAA Public Education Committee also has a Network of State and Provincial Archaeology Education Coordinators, a good place to make contacts for information and planning (www.saa.org/Aboutsaa/Committees/n-penet.html).

EVENTS

Among the more impressive recent developments in archaeology are events specifically aimed at bringing archaeology to the public. Many states now have "Archaeology Months" or "Archaeology Weeks" full of public-oriented events. These might be as simple as lectures or as complicated as participation in experimental archaeology. Favorites include hands-on activities such as letting people try spear throwing, pottery making, or simulated digs. Some include one-day field schools. Iowa, for example, promotes a wide range of activities, usually hosted by local communities but attended by at least one professional archaeologist. The Iowa Archaeology Month website (www.uiowa.edu/~osa/focus/public/iam) provides lots of detail. Wyoming has an "Archaeology Awareness Month" and also promotes archaeology-related events during other times of the year (wyoshpo.state.wy.us/waamindx.htm). Many states have similar activities, and several produce stunning posters to promote the events. At its annual meeting, the SAA hosts a contest for the best poster, and several of the posters have become collector's items.

Archaeological events with a longer history are field schools or volunteer opportunities for lay people. Some archaeologists have raised objections to programs, arguing that we might be training people to loot sites or allowing untrained individuals to dig in potentially important sites. To deal with these issues, many archaeologists include consideration of ethics and request that volunteers spend a minimum number of days on a project. Training takes time, and usually just about the time volunteers have learned the basic skills, they leave.

Archaeology events take money, but you can find grants from state humanities councils and private donors. Events also take staff time and operations resources. On the whole, however, the growing number of these events suggests that archaeologists consider them to be worth the effort.

EXHIBITS AND MUSEUMS

From curiosity cabinets to full-blown permanent galleries, exhibits and museums provide the public with a major point of contact with archaeology. According to the Harris Interactive Poll discussed in chapter 1, fully 88 percent of the public has visited a museum with archaeological content. Museums are a major tourist destination; even small roadside exhibits can pull in visitors. Museums and exhibit design are part of a large and complex discipline, but one in which many archaeologists are employed or involved; truly, saying much in this book about professional museum studies is impossible. At the same time, many of us find ourselves involved in putting up temporary or permanent small exhibits, sometimes related to our CRM or research projects, often on little or no budget, so a few comments may be useful.

Several sources can help if you are faced with building such an exhibit, and you usually don't have time for learning the ins and outs of museum theory. *Museum News*, produced by the American Association of Museums (AAM), is a magazine for professional museum personnel covering a wide range of issues. Similarly, *Curator: The Museum Journal* is mostly for museum professionals, but it provides solid information about exhibition development, studies of visitors, and education. Its "Technical Notes" section can be useful for problem solving.

Hundreds of books are also available. A good place to start is at the AAM Online Bookstore Catalogue (secure.aam-us.org:80/nonmembers/web_store.cgi), which boasts that it contains "the most comprehensive list of titles in the museum profession." Annotations about the content of each volume listed are especially useful.

The web is replete with museum websites, and a search for terms related to building small, temporary exhibits turns up lots of useful sources. From them one can digest several key questions about small exhibits:

- Can a small exhibit give enough information?
- What is the intended life of the exhibit?
- Who has authority over the exhibit and its contents?
- Who is responsible for maintaining the exhibit?
- What are the provisions for security of artifacts and other materials?

As in other aspects of archaeology, making exhibits may benefit from the use of specialists if budgets allow. If a CRM project for a government or large private client has a public component, solicit the agency's or client's advice regarding an exhibit; there may be professional staff who can help.

Whether it's an event or exhibit, all the time, skill, energy, and money you put into it don't mean a thing if no one comes or sees it. Nothing is more disheartening than having no audience. How do you let the public know about archaeology? Archaeology makes a good story, but you have to figure out effective ways to get it to them. That's where the media come in.

11

MEDIA METHOD OR MEDIA MADNESS?

Whether it's a CRM project, a grant from the National Science Foundation, or even a gift from a private donor, most funding for archaeology comes from the public. We just can't afford to fund our own research. As a discipline, we've pondered the best strategy for finding ways to get across the importance of what we do, not only so the public will keep the money coming but also to show them that the past needs to be protected. It's really simple: You have to *work* with the public. Some of us are active supporters of avocational archaeology, whether it's with the local archaeological society, a project allowing volunteer participation, a popular book, or an archaeological website. But working with the public is probably one of the most difficult things we do. How do we find ways to get the public interested at all, let alone educate them about quality archaeological practice?

Thankfully, most people have some level of interest in the past. There is mystery, adventure, and romance in what we do. Archaeology "sells." Many archaeologists who regularly involve the public in their work know this. They also know that media are among the best ways to distribute information. Whether it's a simple local television or radio news spot about an ongoing excavation, a newspaper article, or a full-fledged television documentary, the public does pay attention to what we do.

At the same time, many of us are suspicious of the media. We've probably not had any training in the media, so we really don't know how to handle them very well. Almost every archaeologist has fallen victim to bad reporting. Flawed news stories can easily make you "gun-shy" about all media.

WITH FRIENDS LIKE THE MEDIA, WHO NEEDS ENEMIES?

David Pendergast (1998:15) tells an amusing story from his first press conference about his work at the Mayan Altun Ha site in Belize. After he answered a reporter's question about the use of a string of pearls in front of the face producing crossed eyes in infancy, a headline appeared saying, "Mayas Liked Their Women Cross-eyed." His only comfort was that they spelled his name correctly! My own experience with the Crow Creek Massacre site along the Missouri River in central South Dakota was similar. A *New York Times* reporter asked who had committed the massacre. I hypothesized that nomadic bands had done it, but fearing that he might not know what *nomadic* meant, I used the word *roaming*. In the story, *roaming* unfortunately became *Roman*, with a very uppercase *R*!

Pendergast (1998:15) points out that reporters today are better prepared than their predecessors. They come to interviews with questions better than those most undergraduates ask. Many now come to the story trying to stimulate what he calls fact-based interest. He suggests that the conditions in which we operate with media are greatly improved. The reasons are many but have to do in part with an increased need for news given the expansion of both numbers and types of media outlets. In spite of improvements, he warns that we need to take care in how we present our work and its results. We also need to change our attitudes about media and learn more about them.

ATTITUDES

Archaeologists seem to have a confused relationship with media. We know that we benefit by taking our work to the public, even at the risks we face from misrepresentation of our work, not to mention straightforward reporting errors. Many of us naively used to believe, and probably still do, that we worked in concert with media to bring our projects to the public in an effort to generate greater interest, which in turn would increase support for funding. We were and are grateful that media show interest in us, almost to the degree that we've had an inferiority complex about them. After all, how could anyone be interested in this exotic old stuff?

If anything, the recent Harris poll (Society for American Archaeology 2000) should tell us that such attitudes are very wrong. When 96 percent say there should be laws protecting sites, when 80 percent agree that public funds should be used for archaeology, and when 88 percent have visited a museum with an archeology exhibit, we need to recognize that archaeology has intrinsic value. The reporters recognize this, so why don't we? Archaeology is hardly likely to get to pop culture status, but even a dig in a local area easily raises public curiosity about what is being discovered. Perhaps we need to change our attitudes and strategies about working with media.

LEARN SOMETHING ABOUT MEDIA

The Harris poll also asked respondents about the sources of information from which they learned about archaeology. Although many visit them, fewer than 9 percent chose museums. Television was the most important source at 56 percent, with 33 percent mentioning books and magazines, and 23 percent listing newspapers (Anonymous 1999).

Many archaeologists think they are somewhat sophisticated in terms of media; after all, most probably have done several newspaper and television interviews. Many archaeologists also seem to have at least a slight disdain for media because media are part of pop culture, not something an intellectual elite should worry about. They sometimes don't trust the media because of bad experiences. Thus, the idea of using the media—things like video games, advertising/marketing, broadcast news, television and radio (other than news), movies, newspapers and magazines, music, and the Internet—would probably cause some to choke. Media, however, are a major source for the public's ideas about archaeology, so a wise archaeologist should become truly media-literate.

Media literacy is concerned with developing an informed and critical understanding of the nature of mass media, the techniques they use, and the impact of these techniques. The aim is to increase understanding and enjoyment of how the media work, how they produce meaning, how they are organized, and how they construct reality (see www.media-awareness.ca/eng/).

All media, even popular culture such as archaeological reproductions and trinkets sold to tourists at museum gift shops at archaeological sites, embody points of view, whether or not they are consciously intended. They are based on decisions as broad ranging as what story is to be told and what camera angles might be used, but they lead to questions about how media are organized and how they construct reality. As with images discussed in chapter 6 on visual archaeology, media materials are *not* just reflections of reality. They are preconstructed "products" containing values and ideologies—in our case, about the value of the past and its conservation and preservation. However, most of us are at least aware of this because we understand that we need the media to promote these values. Many archaeologists even recognize that media are mostly a commercial venture, geared to make a profit and controlled by a relatively small number of people, people who are "gatekeepers."

How do these issues play out in media that cover archaeology? As Marshall McLuhan noted years ago, each medium has its own grammar and codifies reality in its own particular way. Different media will report the same event but create different impressions and messages. We need to learn how to work with each to develop the messages we would like to convey regarding the past.

There are lots of opinions and no easy answers as to how to do this, but we do have those on whose experience we can draw. The Society for American Archaeology sponsored a session on media at its 2000 annual meeting, during which four media specialists in archaeology spoke and answered questions. Evan Hadingham represented the PBS science series *Nova*, and Steve Burns represented the Discovery Channel; both are major producers of archaeology television documentaries. Peter Young, the editor of *Archaeology Magazine*, and John Noble Wilford, science writer for the *New York Times*, represented print media. As one might expect, opinions varied, but they agreed on many ideas. One of the important questions was how to know when the story is important enough to "go public," or when does archaeology become news?

FINDING A HOOK

At the SAA seminar, Wilford addressed the issue most directly. One of his most important pieces of advice: Every story needs a "hook," some idea that would first draw the attention of the media and the public. Discoveries that are earlier than we knew or suspected, or new interpretations about them, can be important hooks where a connection can be made to broader issues. New applications of technology or methods can also be a hook, as can something in a discovery that challenges an existing theory or hypothesis or that makes a significant step in solving a question about the past. He noted that almost anything about origins usually provides a good hook. However, he cautioned that almost every story also has to be part of a bigger picture, with meaning for human culture, or part of an active professional debate about the subject. There is nothing wrong with developing hooks that may not be at the core of the ideas that we as scholars think are important, provided they help educate the public about our work

DECIDING WHEN TO GO PUBLIC

When are you ready to go public with a story? This is a difficult call. The story may be so compelling that it becomes public knowledge whether you like it or not, so if your topic is spectacular or controversial, you should be ready at any time. At the SAA seminar, Young discussed the remarkable story of the New York City slave burials and the controversy surrounding them, which raised all sorts of ethical questions about when to go public and what to do once the story breaks. In other cases, you may be able to control the release of the story, such as when an article is about to be released in a peer-reviewed journal or on a website. In such cases, taking a story public may be a matter of when you are ready to face your peers and the media.

As Young noted, having preexisting relationships with the media helps. Although local media reporters are often young and inexperienced, they are usually not "out to get you" and may be your first point of contact to the media outside your area. Hadingham added that in video, it's best if you can make yourself and the project known to producers as early as possible. Many of the seminar presenters noted that as journalists, they do tend to have favorite topics they follow and usually will report.

GETTING NOTICED

If you are preparing to go to the field, are in the field, or are doing something that is likely to be of interest to the public, how do you get noticed? If you figured out what the hook might be and have carefully considered the story in terms of linkages to controversy, new discoveries, and the human side of the story, you are really only part way there.

PUBLIC RELATIONS OFFICES

If the organization for which you work has a public relations (PR) office, as most universities and many larger CRM offices might, media professionals in that office can work with you on presenting your story and getting media attention. Use them if at all possible because they do have experience. They can help you find or clarify the hook if you haven't done so. Experienced public relations people can be worth a great deal to you, so if you find yourself in an organization with a PR office, make yourself known to the staff as soon as you can. Let them know your areas of expertise and the kinds of projects you do.

This can work for you in several ways. If they know you are active and that the things you do are interesting, they'll often contact you on a regular basis. Many PR offices, especially in universities, get calls from media organizations that are looking for experts in areas on which they are doing stories. If you have identified yourself as having a level of expertise in a subject, they'll direct the media to you for comment. If you work well with journalists, you become part of the reporter's contact list, and they may contact you directly. The PR office maintains a list of media contacts, from local to national outlets, and this can be of substantial benefit.

PRESS RELEASES

Press releases are short statements sent to a wide range of media to attract attention to your story. Press releases are not easy to write, so get help from your PR office if you can. If you are on your own, you can still write a good press release. The American Anthropological Association has put together advice on writing a good press release (see sidebar 11.1). Notice that it agrees with the advice from the media professionals at the SAA Ethics meeting.

CHOOSING THE RIGHT LEVEL

Archaeological work often seems very mundane, and thus in your mind it becomes unimportant. For the people of Podunk, however, you as the first archaeologist coming to their town might be big news. You might be amazed to find the editor of the local weekly waiting for you some morning at the survey area. At the other extreme, we

11.1. THE AMERICAN ANTHROPOLOGICAL ASSOCIATION'S *GUIDE TO THE PERFECT PRESS RELEASE*

- The best release is no more than a single page, approximately two hundred words arranged in a maximum of three paragraphs.
- Choose a simple yet compelling title (maximum five words is ideal) to catch the reader's eye. This should capture the most interesting aspect of what you will discuss. As an exercise, imagine yourself in the supermarket checkout line scanning the newspapers and tabloids. What causes you to stop and look twice at one of the headlines? It's probably not the article that begins, "Scientists Find Evidence for Extraterrestrial Life." Instead, you'll probably perk up at the one boldly announcing, "Man in the Moon Waves Back."
- Before beginning to write, ask yourself what is the single most interesting result or aspect of your research—what does this study tell us about ourselves? If your paper is about research in Indonesia, how does it relate to our lives in the United States? Does it tell us something about being human?
- Lead with your best line, rather than building up to it. This is the opposite of writing for an academic audience. Don't expect the reader to bear with you as you first clarify all the whys and wherefores. If details are absolutely necessary in this format, cover them briefly after you have pitched your most appealing sentence.
- Use active tense; avoid the passive and impersonal ("We found . . ." instead of "It was found that . . .").
- Avoid jargon. Visualize explaining the topic to your Aunt Mabel or twelve-year-old nephew. If possible, try the draft on someone outside the field.
- Use at least one concrete example to illustrate your point.
- Give the reporter a reason to ask for more. Although this is a teaser, it is critical to deliver a substantive bottom line. Instead of making vague promises that you will discuss the implications of child rearing in Africa, tell the reader up front that you have observed African mothers to be more nurturing/fulfilled/better prepared than their American sisters—and why.

Adapted from www.aaanet.org/press/relguide.htm. This guide is offered as a public service by the American Anthropological Association and is posted on its website at www.aaanet.org.

sometimes do make interesting discoveries but for all our efforts can't get anyone interested. The problem is one of being too close to what we do to see it in terms of public interest. Another problem is presenting the project in a way that is only of interest to an archaeologist. Thus, one of the main skills to learn is how to pitch the story at the right level.

LOCAL PAPERS

If you are going to do a project in a small town, or even a medium-sized one, making contact with the local paper makes good sense for a lot of reasons. A story in the local paper lets people in the area know who you are and what you are doing. Small-town folks are terribly curious. One of our crews doing a highway relocation survey ventured into a small northwest Iowa town for supplies. The residents are all white, and most are very Dutch Reformed; everybody knows everybody else, and many share the same last name. One of our crew members was African American, and several had beards, a few had tattoos and piercing, and they weren't all that clean. Even in a state car, within minutes of driving into town, they had two police cars following them around and finally "chatting" with them when they stopped at the store.

An added benefit of a story in the paper is that people will often seek you out, many providing you with information about sites in the area. You get to see collections, hear the local stories, and have a chance to interact with folks. For some, especially landowners, such a story may smooth the way for permissions (see Toolkit, volume 2).

Consider writing a series of stories on regional or state archaeologies and releasing them to a wide range of local weekly or daily papers. Klesert (1998) provides excellent resources for how to go about writing for local papers. Set up the stories in ways that allow for quick editing so that a paragraph or two can be quickly eliminated or reduced without dramatically changing the meaning. The odds are that the papers will print the story in some form. If you provide contact information, you may find local collectors at your door or on the phone, ready to give you information on sites in areas where you might do future surveys.

LOCAL TELEVISION AND RADIO

The same benefits can derive from television and radio coverage of a story, but these media outlets usually appear in larger markets and cover a broader region than most local papers. They also tend to be more interested in stories of a bit more importance than some archaeologists looking for sites at the proposed city park shelter. They like controversy, which they see as more newsworthy, because it has that hook. Still, they also like to do stories on discoveries about the past of a region, so if you find some interesting sites, they might do a story, and if you are doing excavations, they are almost bound to cover the project.

Mostly, getting a story done takes a phone call to the station newsroom or news editor. On the downside, they often don't have much background in a subject or the good sense to get the information they need. Radio formats are often different, usually interviews done by phone or in a studio. They are usually not limited to a two- or three-minute story, so they may take the time with you to explore the subject a bit better.

LARGER MARKET MEDIA

Larger markets are more difficult in that they tend to have more news, just for the simple fact of having more people. They generally have better quality in reporting but less time to spend on stories. Here the hook becomes critical to drawing attention. If the market includes a number of communities, the stations may feel an obligation to report something from each of them as news arises, so you may be able to get coverage if your work happens to be the biggest news from that place on a particular day. A better approach is for you to show the importance of a project to the whole market. If you can begin to meet the conditions outlined by the media experts at the SAA panel, you have a better chance of hitting the larger market.

Certainly, the newsworthy stories containing controversy or new, exciting discoveries are an immediate hook, but most archaeology is more mundane. With the right hook, the work might become the subject of a feature. Here is where you need to play on the importance of the work in broader human themes or the application of new technologies or approaches or theories.

For television, the major expansion of cable stations in recent years plays in our favor. For example, at the SAA session, Steve Burns of the Discovery Channel noted that Discovery broadcasts one hundred or more hours of science features and news a week; it needs materials. Because of archaeology's scientific, humanistic, and historical content, archaeology is of possible use to a wide range of specialty cable networks. Burns added that these cable networks often become the first points of contact after a news or feature story appears in print. If they see a story in print, with a hook, the network may actually contact you.

OTHER ADVICE AND CAUTIONS

There is much more to working with the media than getting them to notice you. Most of us just aren't trained to be aware of many of these problems, and learning them through experience is absolutely the hard way.

MASTER THE SOUND BITE

Sound bite is a term you've no doubt heard, where a person says one very short thing, and that becomes the focus of the story. Sound bites work the same way for television, radio, and print media. They are essentially the hook, but in a very direct form, meant to catch the attention of the audience. At a reburial ceremony at Wounded Knee on the Pine Ridge Reservation, Bob Dotson of NBC interviewed me for *Nightly News.* His crew did more than an hour of video on me, and when the segment was aired, I was on for an entire eight seconds of a four-minute piece! Dotson took one pithy statement from me. Since that time, I've worked hard to think about what to say to reporters about stories well ahead of interviews. If I come up with something good, I boil it down into as few catchy words as possible.

To give you an idea of sound bites, my favorites have been "The Crow Creek Massacre changed the way archaeologists viewed Plains Indian warfare" (which is actually a bit too long) and "Indians are from now, not just back then." The latter has been used in papers more often than I can probably count. As silly as sound bites really are, if you consider them ahead of time, you can get a point across quickly.

RESIST TEMPTATION TO CRITICIZE COLLEAGUES

Steve Burns made this point in his discussion at the SAA session, but I've seen colleagues criticize others too often, and I've done so myself a few times. Openly criticizing colleagues in the media puts a question in the mind of the reader/viewer about you. Are you stuck-up—that is, do you think too highly of your own work? Are you being too defensive and using your attack on a colleague to cover weaknesses in your own ideas? You can fairly question ideas of others, but stay away from attacking the person.

PREEMPT WRONG INFORMATION WHERE POSSIBLE

More than once I've given an interview about a field project and had basic information come out all wrong about the site, the age, the cultural complex, and just about anything else a reporter can mess up. One way to handle the problem is to provide basic information about the project ahead of time by doing up a fact sheet about the project. If you are on a CRM project, you can describe the project, the agency funding it, the kind of site or sites found, the cultural complexes, dates associated with them, and artifact types found, with brief explanations of each. In that way your lanceolate projectile point won't become an arrowhead, or its 8,000 B.P. date won't become 8,000 B.C. You may want to include phonetic spellings of difficult names or words to avoid mispronunciations.

AVOID DENIABILITY

If there is an error in reporting, or if you misstated, or if your remarks get taken out of context, there is nothing you can do to make it right. For the record, you should probably report necessary corrections, but whatever you do, your corrections will not get the same coverage as the original story. Sometimes, attempts at corrections can even make things worse.

DEVELOP WAYS TO PRESENT MATERIALS VISUALLY

Steve Burns in the SAA session gave the good advice that archaeologists need to learn how to speak visually—that is, to develop visual imagery through words. For television, he also suggested that archaeologists use available resources to develop real imagery, especially 3D graphics. Pictures do sell a story.

TAKE CHANCES

Burns also noted that we archaeologists are often too cautious. We worry too much about our colleagues or that the media will make us look bad. He didn't mean that we should make statements beyond what our data are capable of supporting. Rather, he meant that conjecture is not always bad, especially if presented that way.

STAY ON POINT

We archeologists tend to be afraid of what colleagues will think, so as we speak to interviewers, we tend to drift away from the story trying to cover our rear ends and get lost in parenthetical asides. Stay on the point, and try to give relatively concise answers. Save your full logic for your articles and books!

ETHICS, CONTEXTS, AND PROFESSIONAL RESPONSIBILITY

The darker side to all of this goes beyond knowing how to present yourself and your work to the media. Archaeologists mostly love what they do; as we sometimes say, archaeology is one of the best things you can do out of bed. We get enthused about what we find and what it means. At the same time, we rarely think about the contemporary repercussions of what we find on the people who are the readers, viewers, and, most important, subjects of our work. We like to think that we are scientists, thoroughly objective in our interpretations. We tout academic freedom; we do not want to feel limited about what we can and cannot say. We need to be cautious. A brief story from Iowa might be instructive (and others could be told):

There has always been controversy about whether syphilis started in the Old World or in the Americas and in which direction it was transmitted. A sexually transmitted disease, syphilis is one of a number of treponemal diseases similar to yaws. Each is difficult to distinguish from the others without specialized tests or solid contexts. After examining some remains from an eight-hundred-year-old burial mound, an Iowa paleopathologist proclaimed to the media that he found evidence of syphilis in Iowa before the Europeans arrived. This made the front page of a statewide paper, and the next day in some Iowa schools, classmates harassed Indian children by telling them, "Your mothers are whores!" That also made front page. The scholar gave his best assessment of the data without thought to its impact; the story is not dissimilar to more recent controversies about evidence of cannibalism at Anasazi sites in the Southwest.

Some in our profession say that we need not be responsible for it—indeed, that it is our job to challenge people's beliefs about themselves and their cultures (see Clark 1996; Mason 1997). Being so naive in the rightness of our own judgments about the past serves no good purpose. We do not need to make archaeology into a cruel discipline. If we reach conclusions that are likely to be harmful to descendant communities, we need to figure out ways to present that information that might make it less damaging. This is not just "political correctness" but respect. We need to carefully contextualize our words to mute the repercussions. In the instance of the syphilis story, for example, the paleopathologist might have mentioned how hard it is to tell syphilis from similar diseases in bone and asked the reporter to emphasize the debate over its origins and the limitations of his findings. We can't control what comes out, but we need to be aware and respectful; that's also part of accountability to the public.

CONCLUSION

Dealing with the media is no easy matter, but it is necessary to what we do. Issues are complex and add another dimension to an already difficult job. With a bit of education in media literacy, you can make the job far easier on yourself. As you have experiences with the media, begin to catalog the incidents so that you can improve your skills. Pay attention to what works well and what doesn't. As with writing and speaking, practice doing some of the skills discussed in this chapter, such as writing a press release or giving an interview. Have a colleague or friends critique your performance. Prepare a handout for reporters who might appear at your next project. Working with the media can actually be fun and rewarding, but if you aren't ready, you may find yourself in a small public relations fiasco or, at very least, embarrassed. So much happens very quickly in the media, so the bad that happens is usually forgotten quickly.

Other forces, affecting both the media with which we deal and all the ways we present the past, will change much of what we do in the future. Most of these forces have to do with new technologies as ways of delivering content to our publics. That's our final topic in chapter 12.

12

THE FUTURE OF PRESENTING THE PAST

The shift in ways to think about presenting the past over the past decade has been rapid and remarkable. Early adopters of the World Wide Web will probably recall looking at information about archaeology on the web late in 1994, a mere decade ago. At last estimate, some twenty million new websites pop up a year, but there's no real way of knowing. A surprising number of them, with a wide range of quality, contain information about archaeology.

CD-ROMs preceded the web a bit, but they were primarily for games and a few educational products, mostly commercial ventures. Archaeology has taken a long time to start using them. Still, at the exhibit room and in publishers' flyers at the 2002 SAA meeting, I counted about a dozen that used archaeological sites and data as a primary component of the disk.

DVDs have also become readily available, allowing vastly more data storage for inclusion of large numbers of images, video, and sound. Development of new media seems to come quickly, posing new challenges.

New technologies always seem to fascinate archaeologists in other areas of their work, so I've been a bit surprised that we have not picked up on the use of these new ways of presenting material to both colleagues and the public as quickly as I thought we would. One reason we've been slow is that using new technologies requires learning new hardware and software. Another, however, is that many of us are trained to think in the very linear ways that writing promotes. The web and CD-ROMs promote a different way of seeing and presenting materials, one that is multilinear. Although there is an underlying structure to what has been called hypermedia, a user can move around in the medium easily, and it is vastly more dependent on sound, images, and interactivity than any medium we have yet produced in archaeology.

To use the new technologies, we are faced with problems of design, computer programming, and production of audio and video. Most of us just don't have the training and certainly don't have the time to deal with substantial learning curves in each element of the production. We are comfortable with the idea of controlling content, but not how to design or produce it for the new media.

What is necessary to produce the highest-quality hypermedia is a team of people, with each member a specialist in one or two elements. As discussed in chapter 7, one may need to add a graphic designer, a video specialist, an audio specialist, and a computer programmer—more! Every team member adds greater costs to the project. However, producing a website, CD-ROM, or DVD can be done with reasonably skilled nonspecialists. The basics are really pretty simple.

ARCHAEOLOGY ON THE WEB

If you haven't used the World Wide Web to look up information about archaeology, you are probably really unusual, a practicing Luddite, or a real technophobe. Most who have used the web understand its potential for providing information to both your colleagues and archaeology's other publics:

- It allows you to quickly combine images, text, sound, and video.
- It is certainly cheaper than printing a book or multiple copies of a report.
- It lets anyone in the world with web access see your materials quickly.

WEB BASICS

The fundamentals of website construction are easy. To use the web, you need a computer with some level of access to the Internet, a web browser, a web server, and a way to do HTML (hypertext markup language). These are explained in lots of books, and building websites can be accomplished with lots of different tools, including your own word processor, which probably offers an option of saving text files as a web page. To do exactly what you want may be more complicated and so may require learning a WYSIWYG (what you see is what you get) web-editing program or learning to do HTML "on the fly."

DEVELOPING WEB APPEAL

You can't use the web for very long without seeing something you'd like to have on your own website. Many fancy animations, sounds, and image placement require special programs for you to construct and may require a web browser plug-in. Plug-ins are usually free, but the programs to design what the plug-in is used to see are usually not. Some browsers come with many of the plug-ins already installed; download and install new ones as you need them. Some of these specialized programs produce what is essentially eye candy to draw in your audience, but others provide essential services.

One good example of an essential plug-in is Adobe Acrobat Reader because many organizations, especially government agencies, put documents on the web that way, including CRM reports, requests for proposals, and the like. Acrobat Reader reads .pdf (portable document files), which are facsimile copies of documents you produce with your word processor. To create .pdf files may require the installation of the full Adobe Acrobat program, which works in tandem with common word processors. Many fancy elements on the web can be done with high-end HTML editors. Forms, for example, are easy to create, but they require your web server to have special programs. These programs have been written in Perl, C++, or some other language and get called into and used by your web page through cgi (common gateway interface). Other fancy stuff is programmed in Java, a language developed especially for the web; Javascript is similar. Some high-end HTML editors will help you by writing the program for what you want to do.

Most of us don't want to get involved in such detailed programming, but we don't mind fiddling with code someone else has developed. One easy approach is to see a program you like on a website, "borrow" the code, and then modify it to your needs. That takes minimal programming experience. For some eye candy, you will need to buy a program, learn it, and create what you need.

As the web has proliferated, so have the tools. If you are going to use them, consider their costs and benefits in both time and money for what you hope the user will get out of it. Another concern is that until broadband Internet is available to more users, some of your creations will only be accessible to relatively narrow audiences. There are a few tools that archaeologists can use effectively.

VRML (VIRTUAL REALITY MODELING LANGUAGE)

Virtual reality is common in video games, but a number of archaeologists have written about it or applied it to websites and CD-ROMs. *Virtual reality* is the creation of a facsimile of the real thing, sometimes with three dimensions but as often with two dimensions on the video or computer screen. To build virtual reality is complex but certainly holds promise for archaeology.

A VRML document takes the form of a human-readable text file describing a three-dimensional scene. This text file is a list of commands that tell the computer to place objects of given sizes and colors at specific locations within a virtual world. The benefit of VRML is that lots of data can be represented visually in ways that allow you to see patterns that might not be apparent in a spreadsheet of numbers or measurements. In analysis of data, this feature can help spot problems with data shortage or weakness, or it may provide insight to organization or linkages of data. For presentation of some data, virtual reality is a major plus to help those not familiar with the data "see" what you are writing or talking about.

CRM will find VRML-generated data output to be a useful tool for predictive modeling. GIS 3D projections are already a form of virtual reality, and "fly-through" can make site predictive models seem much more real to project managers. VRML is also a way to make data meaningful to nonspecialists; for example, a recent article by Gummerman and Dean (2000) discusses the application for Anasazi archaeology. Vince and Garside-Neville (1997) provide a summary as well, but they give a somewhat less positive view due to speed and file sizes. The electronic journal *Internet Archaeology* (intarch/york.ac.uk/) presents several excellent examples of VRML use, so peruse the issue's table of contents.

One of the early models on the web was that of Chetro Ketl (Kanter 2001). If you've not seen VRML, this is a good place to start, but you will need to download a few plug-ins onto your computer if you don't already have them.

DIGITAL AUDIO AND DIGITAL VIDEO

If you've used the web, you've probably already encountered audio. Digital audio is relatively simple. You can prepare digital audio if you can connect a microphone to your computer's sound card. For short audio files, where great clarity is not all that important (some music and most spoken voice), you literally can speak or play right into the microphone. Most computers come with a program to allow you to do simple sound editing to help clean the sound up a bit, but for music, where clarity is important, or for mixing, you may want to use a specialized program that handles the growing range of audio file types.

As already discussed in chapter 6, video can easily be adapted to use on the web. The core issues in digital video use on the web are file size and bandwidth. Video file size is extremely large, so compression of files is necessary (which is why most video doesn't fill the whole screen), as is sampling, which decreases the number of frames per second (fps). The lower the fps, the more jerky the video looks. *Bandwidth* is essentially the amount of information that can move from computer to computer in a certain amount of time. Slow telephone modems have a much smaller bandwidth than cable modems, for example, and this affects the speed at which the user gets to see the material from your website. For people with low bandwidth, the World Wide Web becomes the World Wide Wait!

Streaming media uses specialized file formats and compression to allow the video and audio to begin playing as soon as they start downloading. This lets the user see/hear immediately, and compression doesn't have to be so severe. Bandwidth still has an impact.

SOME PROBLEMS WITH USING THE WEB (AND A FEW FIXES)

For all the benefits the web brings for relatively low-cost presentations of archaeological materials and easy access to them, it also can create problems. All of them are issues you need to consider if you decide to use the web to deliver archaeological materials to professional colleagues or the public.

- *Problem 1: The web is more ephemeral than printed materials.* Websites tend to go away more quickly than most of us like. The medium is constantly changing, so that what a site had on it yesterday may not be on it today. If sites are maintained, content that was once featured may now be buried or removed from the site. If you find material on a website that is very useful to you, you may want to save the particular page or site on disk or perhaps even print it. If you want to save the whole website, that's also easy using purchased programs, shareware, or freeware.

- *Problem 2: Materials on the web are not peer reviewed.* Anyone with resources can put up a website to say just about anything. The web contains a wealth of junk, but you might remember that most libraries do as well. Many journals and even some monographs on the web are starting to be peer reviewed, which raises their credibility. Even if not peer reviewed, they may well be put up by a competent archaeologist and edited by competent editors. As with any material you use as a scholar, you need to know how to evaluate websites. You'll find lots of advice about this on the web itself and perhaps need to consider how this advice needs to be modified to suit archaeological information. Alexander and Tate (1999) offer excellent suggestions for both evaluating websites and providing users with ways to evaluate your own materials.

- *Problem 3: Flash sometimes takes precedence over content.* Websites can now do so much with graphics, sound, and video that site layout, art, and action sometimes take precedence over content. If you are on a slow connection, this becomes profoundly annoying. At the same time, be aware that web users tend to be younger and that many have grown up with the eye candy of television, MTV, and video games. "Flash" can bring attention to your website, but too much becomes a problem. One good way to figure out what you should put on your site is to look at others you find well organized and attractive, and then design a site like them. In truth, much beyond simple web layout might best be left to specialists in graphics and web design.

    Remember, though, that on the web, *content is king*, no matter what might be possible in terms of the software and eye candy. Less is probably best in terms of the fancy design, but at the same time, websites with text alone defeat the purpose of the medium. A good mix of media is fine, but don't go overboard.

- *Problem 4: Some websites are very hard to navigate.* If you have visited some websites with lots of materials, you can sometimes quickly get lost in the many pages of information provided. Good sites provide good navigation tools.

- *Problem 5: The real cost of the web comes in maintaining the website!* If your website contains any content that can change outside of your control, your single biggest cost will be in maintaining the site. The costs mostly come in time, not money, trying to keep content current. This will especially be the case if your website contains lots of links to other sites. You'll be vastly happier if you provide original content and as few links to other sites as possible. If your site contains active data such as databases, these can also take a great deal of time to maintain. Whatever the complexity of your website, count on the fact that you'll need to provide regular maintenance.

CD-ROMs AND DVDs

CD-ROMs actually appeared shortly before the web, but they are fundamentally the same. They both use hypermedia, linking a range of audio, graphics, video, and text about a subject. The major difference is that a CD-ROM resides in your own computer. Up to seven hundred megabytes (MB) of files get stored on a CD-ROM disk rather than on a web server. In contrast, DVD-ROMs hold a minimum of 4.7 gigabytes (GB) of information. This huge capacity can hold a full-length movie and then some. The way they work is the same, but they sometimes require different players.

Designing a CD or DVD is much the same as designing a website, with a few added complexities because they are stand-alone products. The web is mostly platform-independent, but CDs and DVDs are not. You must decide whether to make your product playable by Windows, Macintosh, or both. Public schools tend to use Macintosh systems heavily, so you'll probably want to provide for both. Fortunately, this is mostly a matter of adding easily acquired software to make your program run on each platform.

One simple way around this is to use HTML, which is platform-independent, to set up a website, and then transfer the whole thing to the CD/DVD. To make the product work, you need to instruct users to open a web browser and which file name to type in the location/URL/address line of the browser. Once they've done that, they are on their way. If they do this with a live Internet connection, you can even include links to external websites.

You might ask why you'd want to put the product on a CD/DVD instead of the web. The answers are simple:

- There will be no problems with down servers.
- Slow web connections are nonexistent.

- Bandwidth is not a concern.
- Vastly more material can be included than on most websites.

If you choose not to use an HTML-based approach, you'll want to acquire a multimedia authoring program to build your CD/DVD. Most have a steep learning curve, but they are worth the trouble for the amount of control you get in combining and sequencing your materials.

STORYBOARDING: A CRUCIAL CONCEPT FOR WEBSITES AND CDs/DVDs

When you learned how to write, your teachers probably taught you the use of outlines, a way of organizing your thoughts before you put them onto paper. In a sense, the outline keeps you from getting lost in a maze of ideas, citations, illustrations, and other items you'd like in your document. Storyboarding is a similar concept but borrowed from filmmaking. In the case of the web, CD-ROMs, and DVDs, storyboards help you keep your files, images, and direction in place. Guthrie (2000) provides the following storyboarding steps:

1. Define the purpose of your page.
2. Identify the audience for this page (primary, secondary, or other).
3. Choose the main heading for the page.
4. Identify major categories of information that will go on your page, and place related information in these categories.
5. Determine how you will link information. Identify which links are relative and which are absolute.
6. Decide what graphics and images you will use (your .jpg and .gif files).
7. Plan how you will provide navigation through the pages (e.g., buttons, bars, text, bottom of the page, side of the page, or top of the page).
8. Draw a simple sketch depicting how the pages or topics link to one another. (For additional information, see the storyboarding bibliography compiled by Marie Wallace at www.llrx.com/columns/sbbiblio.htm.)

A growing body of professional computer software can help with storyboarding, but it tends to be expensive. You might do just as well with a notepad. Take it from lots of bad experience: Storyboarding can really help your product!

INTERACTIVITY: BRINGING THE PAST TO LIFE

The strength of using new media for presenting the past is that they can bring the past to life by allowing the user to interact in ways that text and a few pictures cannot do. Hypermedia provide ways for an individual to make choices about where to go, what to see, and in what order. Words alone can fire imaginations, but not in the same way. Interactivity helps the user understand the complexities of ancient cultural systems and many of the processes at work in them. Interactivity is definitely nonlinear.

The problem with being trained in a discipline is that you sometimes have trouble thinking outside the box. For archaeologists trained in linear approaches to discovering and interpreting the past, this is a problem. If you intend to design new media, you'll need to train yourself to think in different ways. One good way to get a feel for this is to try lots of video games and educational programs just to understand the approach. There are even some featuring archaeology (Watrall 2002). Certainly, you need to try to see things the way your audiences might. See what's out there, and consider the possibilities.

Let me go out on what is a rather secure limb: Print media are not going to go away, but the web and its descendants will be the future for delivering archaeological materials to colleagues and our publics. There is plenty of room for CDs/DVDs, and in the near term, you'll see a great deal of experimentation using virtual reality, streaming audio and video, and a host of other applications. With wider distribution of broadband web access, especially Internet 2, much more will be possible, so much so that predicting what you'll see on the web in a decade is like trying to predict what you'll find when you put a test pit in an archaeological site. The key for your success in using the web or any other new media will be your own creativity and your budget.

We shouldn't be afraid of these developments or let our tradition of emphasizing print media stand in the way of experimentation and adoption of new technologies. Thankfully, there are always a few who push the edges. Over the past decade, several challenging articles have appeared in the *SAA Bulletin* as part of a "Net Works" column, helping expand the horizon for presenting the past. New technologies bring new issues and problems, and colleagues are addressing them. For example, the SAA recently published a collection of papers, *Delivering Archaeological Information Electronically* (Carroll 2002), that addresses a range of issues from peer review to archiving of materials.

CONCLUSION

This book began with a discussion of archaeologists' ethical obligations to the past, and it will end that way. Stewardship, however it gets defined, is complex and underpins everything we do. It is not just a matter of protecting the physical remains of the past or creating an intellectual record of the past. If we agree that it is a public heritage, then we have to make the past *public;* that is, we have to make what we do "transparent" in terms of the ways we do and think about things. We have to let people know about what we find but also, as important, what we believe to be its impacts for their lives. This is a profound responsibility. If the past is a public heritage, then archaeologists are partners with the public as stewards of that heritage. Presenting the past is part of that partnership. Do it well, do it creatively, and do it responsibly.

APPENDIX

SOME ARCHAEOLOGY
JOURNALS ON THE WEB

Many Archaeology journals have associated websites. Some list tables of contents, and some have the same articles as the print editions. URLs do change, so if the links listed here do not work, use a search engine to try to find the site.

Aerial Archaeology Newsletter: www.nmia.com/~jaybird/AANewsletter/
African American Archaeology Newsletter: www.mindspring.com/ ~wheaton/NSA.html
African Archaeology Review: www.plenum.com
American Antiquity: www.saa.org/Publications/AmAntiq/amantiq .html
Andean Past: kramer.ume.maine.edu/~anthrop/AndeanP.html
Anthropology Today (some archaeology): lucy.ukc.ac.uk/rai/
Antiquity: intarch.ac.uk/antiquity
Archaeoastronomy & Ethnoastronomy News: www.wam.umd.edu/ ~tlaloc/archastro/
Archaeological Dialogues: archweb.LeidenUniv.nl/ad/home_ad.html
Archaeology Ireland Magazine: slarti.ucd.ie/pilots/archaeology/
Archaeology Magazine: www.he.net/~archaeol/index.html
Assemblage (The Sheffield Graduate Journal of Archaeology): www.shef.ac.uk/uni/union/susoc/assem/index.html
At the Edge: www.gmtnet.co.uk/indigo/edge/atehome.htm
Berkeley Archaeology: www.qal.berkeley.edu/arf/
British Archaeology: britac3.britac.ac.uk/cba/ba/ba.html
Bulletin of Information on Computing in Anthropology: lucy.ukc.ac .uk/bicaindex.html

CRM: www.cr.nps.gov/crm

Cultural Anthropology Methods (CAM): www.lawrence.edu/~bradleyc/cam.html

Current Anthropology (some archaeology): www.artsci.wustl.edu/~anthro/ca

Current Archaeology: www.archaeology.co.uk

Forum Archaeologiae (Austrian Journal of Archaeology): allergy.hno.akh-wien.ac.at/forum/

Glasgow University Archaeological Research Division (GUARD) Digest Reports: www.gla.ac.uk/Acad/Archaeology/guard/guard

Internet Archaeology: intarch.york.ac.uk

Journal of Field Archaeology: jfa-www.bu.edu

Journal of Material Culture: www.sagepub.co.uk/journals/details/mcu.html

KMT: A Modern Journal of Ancient Egypt: www.sirius.com/~reeder/kmt.html

Latin American Antiquity: www.saa.org/Publications/LatAmAnt/latamant.html

Midcontinental Journal of Archaeology: www.uiowa.edu/~osa/publica/mcja/mcja.htm

Online Archaeology: avebury.arch.soton.ac.uk/Journal/journal.html

SAA Bulletin: www.sscf.ucsb.edu/SAABulletin

 **REFERENCES**

Addington, Lucile R.
1986   *Lithic Illustration: Drawing Flaked Stone Artifacts for Publication.* University of Chicago Press, Chicago.

Adkins, Lasley, and Roy A. Adkins
1989   *Archaeological Illustration.* Cambridge University Press, Cambridge.

Alexander, Janet E., and Marsha Ann Tate
1999   *Web Wisdom: How to Evaluate and Create Information Quality on the Web.* Erlbaum, Mahwah, N.J.

Allen, Mitch
2002   Reaching the Hidden Audience: Ten Rules for the Archaeological Writer. In *Public Benefits of Archaeology,* edited by Barbara J. Little, pp. 244–51. University Press of Florida, Gainesville.

Anonymous
1999   Tuning in on Public Opinion. *Common Ground,* Winter 1999:5.
2001   Photographing Archaeological Sites. *American Archaeology* 5(1):21–28.

Armstrong, Douglas V.
1985   Maps. In *The Student's Guide to Archaeological Illustrating,* edited by B. Dillon, pp. 27–42. University of California–Los Angeles Institute of Archaeology Archaeological Research Tools, Volume 1, Los Angeles.
2001   *Evaluating Web Resources.* www2.widener.edu/Wolfgram-Memorial-Library/webevaluation/webeval.htm. Viewed April 20, 2001.

Bahn, Paul, and Bill Tidy
    1999   *Disgraceful Archaeology or Things You Shouldn't Know about the History of Mankind*. Tempus Publishing, Charleston, S.C.

Baxter, Jane E.
    1996   Getting Graphic! Making an Effective Poster. *SAA Bulletin* 14(5):9, 31.

Becker, Howard S.
    1986   *Writing for Social Scientists: How to Start and Finish Your Thesis, Book, or Article*. University of Chicago Press, Chicago.

Bender, Susan J., and George S. Smith (eds.)
    2000   *Teaching Archaeology in the 21st Century*. Society for American Archaeology, Washington, D.C.

Brodribb, Conant
    1971   *Drawing Archaeological Finds*. Association Press, New York.

Bronowski, Jacob
    1973   *The Ascent of Man*. Little, Brown, Boston.

Carroll, Mary S. (ed.)
    2002   *Delivering Archaeological Information Electronically*. Society for American Archaeology, Washington, D.C.

Clark, G. A.
    1996   NAGPRA and the Demon-Haunted World. *SAA Bulletin* 14(5):3.

December, John, and Susan Katz
    1996   Abstracts. Rensselaer Polytechnic Institute: The Writing Center. www.rpi.edu/llc/writecenter/web/text/abstracts.html. Viewed April 16, 2001.

Deloria, Vine
    1995   *Red Earth, White Lies: Native Americans and the Myth of Scientific Fact*. Scribner's, New York.

Dillon, Brian
    1985   Introduction. In *The Student's Guide to Archaeological Illustrating*, edited by B. Dillon, pp. 3–8. Archaeological Research Tools, Volume 1. University of California at Los Angeles, Institute of Archaeology.

Dorrell, Peter
    1989   *Photography in Archaeology and Conservation*. Cambridge University Press, Cambridge.

Ducette, Martin
    1999   *Digital Video for Dummies*. Wiley, New York.

Dvorak, John
2001 Closing in on Perfection. *PC Magazine* 20(6):79.

Eiseley, Loren
1971 *The Night Country.* Scribner's, New York.

Fagan, Brian
2002 I Am So Tired of Jargon and Narrow Teaching. . . . *SAA Archaeological Record* 2(2):5–7.

Gonick, Larry
1990 *The Cartoon History of the Universe,* Volumes 1–7, *From the Big Bang to Alexander the Great.* Doubleday, New York.

Gummerman, George J., and Jeffrey Dean
2000 Artificial Anasazi. *Discovering Archaeology* 2(2):44–51.

Guthrie, Sally
2000 *Storyboarding.* web.utk.edu/~sguthrie/j416/storyboard.htm. Viewed April 23, 2001.

Halsey, John R.
1991 "State Secrets": The Protection and Management of Archaeological Site Information in Michigan. In *Ethics and Professional Anthropology,* edited by C. Fluehr-Lobban, pp. 115–19. University of Pennsylvania Press, Philadelphia.

Hart, Russell, and Dan Richards
1998 *Photography for Dummies.* Wiley, New York.

Hartley, L. P.
1953 *The Go Between.* Hamilton, London.

Heider, Karl
1976 *Ethnographic Film.* Austin, University of Texas Press.
2001 *Seeing Anthropology: Cultural Anthropology Through Film.* Allyn and Bacon, Boston.

Heizer, Robert F., and John A. Graham
1967 *A Guide to Field Methods in Archaeology: Approaches to the Anthropology of the Dead.* National Press, Palo Alto, Calif.

Hester, Thomas R., Harry J. Shafer, and Kenneth L. Feder
1997 *Fields Methods in Archaeology.* Mayfield, Mountain View, Calif.

Houk, Brett A., and Bruce K. Moses
1998 Scanning Artifacts: Using a Flatbed Scanner to Image Three-Dimensional Objects. *SAA Bulletin* 16(3):36–39.

Howell, Carol L., and Warren Blanc
1992 *A Practical Guide to Archaeological Photography.* University of California at Los Angeles, Institute of Archaeology.

Jameson, John H., Jr. (ed.)
1997 *Presenting Archaeology to the Public: Digging for Truths.* AltaMira, Walnut Creek, Calif.

Kantner, John
2001 Sipapu-Anasazi Great House Model. sipapu.gsu.edu/kinshow/ kin.tliish.html. Viewed April 16, 2001.

King, Julie Adair
1999 *Digital Photography for Dummies.* Wiley, New York.

Klesert, Anthony L.
1998 You Too Can Write Good: Writing about Archaeology for Local Newspapers. *SAA Bulletin* 16(3):40–41.

Lynott, Mark, and Alison Wylie (eds.)
1995 *Ethics in American Archaeology: Challenges for the 1990s.* Society for American Archaeology, Washington, D.C.

Macaulay, David
1979 *Motel of the Mysteries.* Houghton Mifflin, New York.

Mason, Ronald J.
1997 Letter to the Editor, *SAA Bulletin* 15(1):3.

McPherron, Shannon P., and Harold L. Dibble
2002 *Using Computers in Archaeology: A Practical Guide.* McGraw-Hill, Mayfield, Boston.

Molyneaux, Brian L.
1997 Introduction: The Cultural Life of Images. In *The Cultural Life of Images: Visual Representation in Archaeology,* edited by B. Molyneaux, pp. 1–10. Routledge, London.

National Park Service
2000 National Archeological Database Reports. www.cast.uark .edu/products/NADB/nadb.mul.html. Viewed April 4, 2001.

Neiman, Fraser D.
1994 A Poster Primer: A Few Tips for Planning Your Poster Session. *SAA Bulletin* 12(1):13–14.

Pendegast, David
1998 The Bedfellows Are Less Strange These Days: The Changing Relationship between Archaeologists and the Media. *SAA Bulletin* 16(5):15–16.

Piggott, Stuart
   1979   *Antiquity Depicted: Aspects of Archaeological Illustration.* Thames and Hudson, London.

Renfrew, Colin, and Paul Bahn
   1996   *Archaeology: Theories, Methods and Practice.* Thames and Hudson, London.

Rick, John
   1999   Digital Still Cameras and Archaeology. *SAA Bulletin* 17(1):37–41.

Rick, John, and Dakin Hart
   1997   Panoramic Virtual Reality and Archaeology. *SAA Bulletin* 15(5):14–19.

Smardz, Karolyn E., and Shelley J. Smith (eds.)
   2000   *The Archaeology Education Handbook: Sharing the Past with Kids.* AltaMira, Walnut Creek, Calif.

Society for American Archaeology
   1992   Editorial Policy, Information for Authors, and Style Guide for *American Antiquity* and *Latin American Antiquity. American Antiquity* 57:749–70 and www.saa.org/Publications/StyleGuide/saaguide.pdf. Viewed May 28, 2002.
   1996   Principles of Archaeological Ethics. www.saa.org/Aboutsaa/Ethics/prethic.html. Viewed April 23, 2002.
   1999   *Teaching Archaeology in the 21st Century: Promoting a National Dialogue.* www.saa.org/Education/Curriculum/principles1.html. Viewed May 28, 2002.
   2000   Poll Finds Public Support of Archaeology. www.saa.org/Pubrel/publiced-poll.html. Viewed May 28, 2002.

Vince, Alan, and Sandra Garside-Neville
   1997   Publishing multimedia in archaeology. *Internet Archaeology.* intarch.york.ac.uk/news/eva97.html. Viewed April 23, 2001.

Watrall, Ethan
   2002   Interactive Entertainment as Public Archaeology. *SAA Archaeological Record* 2(2):37–39.

Whittaker, John
   1992   Hard Times at Lizard Man. *Archaeology* 45(4):56–58.

Zimmerman, Larry J.
   1985   *Peoples of Prehistoric South Dakota.* University of Nebraska Press, Lincoln.
   1986   Redwing. *Anthropology and Humanism Quarterly* 11(1):8–9.

1995   Regaining Our Nerve: Ethics, Values and Transforming Archae-
        ology. In *Ethics in American Archaeology: Challenges for the
        1990s*, edited by M. Lynott and A. Wylie, pp. 64–67. Society for
        American Archaeology, Washington, D.C.
2001   Usurping Native American Voice. In *The Future of the Past: Ar-
        chaeologists, Native Americans and Repatriation*, edited by
        Tamara L. Bray, pp. 169–84. Garland, New York.

Zimmerman, Larry J., and Lawrence E. Bradley
1993   The Crow Creek Massacre, Initial Coalescent Warfare and Spec-
        ulations about the Genesis of Extended Coalescent. *Plains An-
        thropologist*, 38(145):215–26.

Zimmerman, Larry J., Steve Dasovich, Mary Engstrom, and Lawrence
Bradley
1994   Listening to the Teachers: Warnings about the Use of the Ar-
        chaeological Agenda in the Classroom. In *The Presented Past:
        Archaeology, Museums and Public Education*, edited by
        P. Stone and B. Molyneaux, pp. 359–74. Routledge, London.

INDEX

ABOUT THE AUTHOR AND SERIES EDITORS

Larry J. Zimmerman is the head of the Archaeology Department of the Minnesota Historical Society. He served as an adjunct professor of anthropology and visiting professor of American Indian and Native Studies at the University of Iowa from 1996 to 2002 and as chair of the American Indian and Native Studies Program from 1998 to 2001. He earned his Ph.D. in anthropology at the University of Kansas in 1976. Teaching at the University of South Dakota for twenty-two years, he left there in 1996 as Distinguished Regents Professor of Anthropology.

While in South Dakota, he developed a major CRM program and the University of South Dakota Archaeology Laboratory, where he is still a research associate. He was named the University of South Dakota Student Association Teacher of the Year in 1980, given the Burlington Northern Foundation Faculty Achievement Award for Outstanding Teaching in 1986, and granted the Burlington Northern Faculty Achievement Award for Research in 1990. He was selected by Sigma Xi, the Scientific Research Society, as a national lecturer from 1991 to 1993, and he served as executive secretary of the World Archaeological Congress from 1990 to 1994. He has published more than three hundred articles, CRM reports, and reviews and is the author, editor, or coeditor of fifteen books, including *Native North America* (with Brian Molyneaux, University of Oklahoma Press, 2000) and *Indians and Anthropologists: Vine Deloria, Jr., and the Critique of Anthropology* (with Tom Biolsi, University of Arizona Press, 1997). He has served as the editor of *Plains Anthropologist* and the *World Archaeological Bulletin* and as the associate editor of

American Antiquity. He has done archaeology in the Great Plains of the United States and in Mexico, England, Venezuela, and Australia. He has also worked closely with a wide range of American Indian nations and groups.

William Green is the director of the Logan Museum of Anthropology and an adjunct professor of anthropology at Beloit College, Beloit, Wisconsin. He has been active in archaeology since 1970. Having grown up on the south side of Chicago, he attributes his interest in archaeology and anthropology to the allure of the exotic (i.e., rural) and a driving urge to learn the unwritten past, abetted by the opportunities available at the city's museums and universities. His first fieldwork was on the Mississippi River bluffs in western Illinois. Although he also worked in Israel and England, he returned to Illinois for several years of survey and excavation. His interests in settlement patterns, ceramics, and archaeobotany developed there. He received his master's degree from the University of Wisconsin at Madison and then served as Wisconsin SHPO staff archaeologist for eight years. After obtaining his Ph.D. from the University of Wisconsin at Madison in 1987, he served as state archaeologist of Iowa from 1988 to 2001, directing statewide research and service programs including burial site protection, geographic information, publications, contract services, public outreach, and curation. His main research interests focus on the development and spread of native agriculture. He has served as editor of the *Midcontinental Journal of Archaeology* and *The Wisconsin Archeologist;* has published articles in *American Antiquity, Journal of Archaeological Research,* and other journals; and has received grants and contracts from the National Science Foundation, National Park Service, Iowa Humanities Board, and many other agencies and organizations.